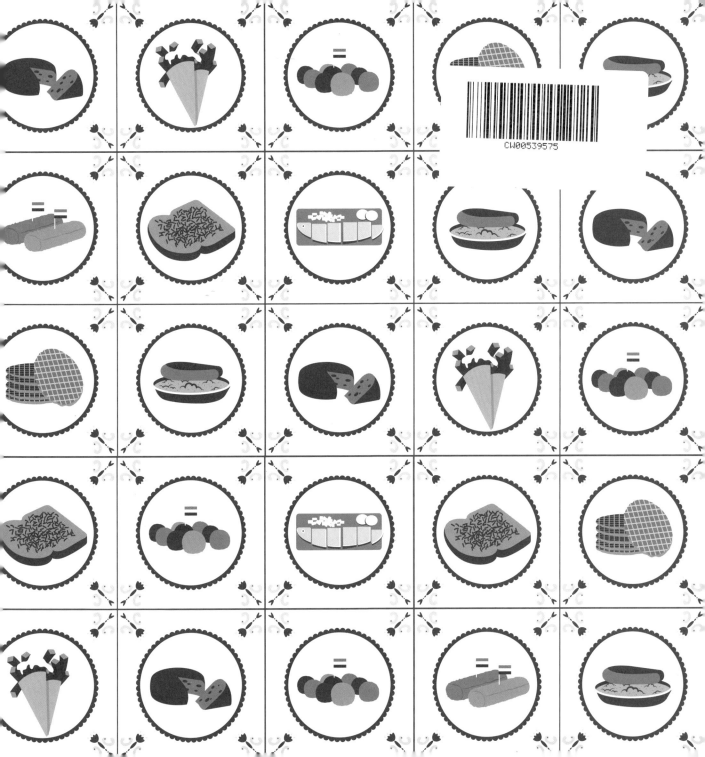

presents

Stuff Dutch People Eat

Copyright © 2016 by Colleen Geske

All rights reserved. No part of this publication may be reproduced, stored in a retrieval system, or transmitted, in any form or in any means – by electronic, mechanical, photocopying, recording or otherwise – without prior written permission.

Words by Colleen Geske

Production by Moses Faleafaga

Published in the Netherlands by Stuff Dutch People Like

Some of the material in this book may have originally appeared, in different form, on the popular blog StuffDutchPeopleLike.com

Photo & other credits can be found on page 164

ISBN 978-90-821336-3-9

Printed in the EU

10 9 8 7 6 5 4 3 2 1

www.stuffdutchpeoplelike.com
www.facebook.com/stuffdutchpeoplelike
www.instagram.com/stuffdutchpeoplelike
www.twitter.com/stuffdutchlike

For media inquiries, corporate & volume sales or any other request, please contact us at
hello@stuffdutchpeoplelike.com

Dedication

This book is dedicated to my wonderful hubby, who has made 98% of my meals since the day we met. Thanks for feeding me and keeping me alive all these years. Who would have thought we'd make a cookbook together? If you don't mind, I'll remain our 'special events chef' and leave the daily bits to you. xo

STUFF DUTCH PEOPLE EAT

A celebration of the delightfully delicious food Dutch people eat!

by Colleen Geske

Contents

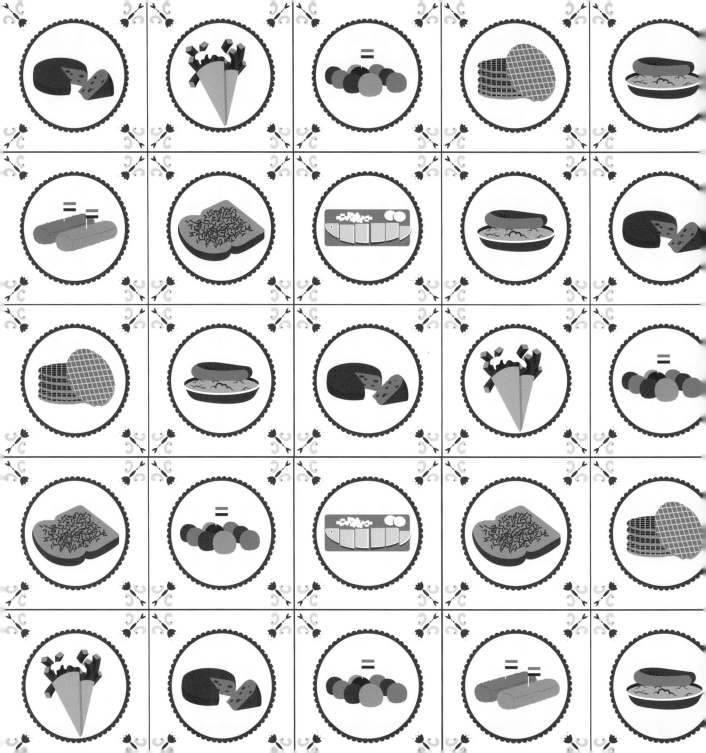

A funny thing happens when you start blogging about Dutch culture. Suddenly people want to hear more; they interview, they question, they ask, and then they invite you to sit on panels and stand in front of crowds to talk about "what Dutch people are really like". It's utterly odd and fascinating at the same time. You become some sort of informal 'expert' on a subject you were, in fact, only trying to better understand. And so, you share your 2 cents for what it's worth, and carry on...

...that is until the "sometimes random yet alway fun" questions start pouring in: What should I wear to a Dutch job interview? What does my Dutch mother-in-law mean when she says such-and-such? How can I find a Dutch husband? Where can I buy a poster of Dutch people riding bikes in the rain? How do I tell my Dutch colleague I have a crush on her? I'm 5'1" (154cm) am I too short to live in Holland? Can you help me find a certain Jaap de Boer?

So you do your best to point John from America in the right direction to locate his long-lost-Dutch-Grandpa's-sister's-cousin. And you answer that, "No, sorry you haven't met that other Canadian girl, Karen, who also happens to live in the Netherlands" and "Yes, your Dutch mother-in-law does indeed sound a bit too direct".

And then, for some reason, people start sending you recipes. Yes, recipes! Random, right? And as more recipes start flowing in, so do the endless stream of "recipe related" questions: How do you make *appelflappen*? Can you publish some genuine Dutch recipes? What is the best way to make *erwtensoep*? Do you have a recipe for *Oliebollen*? *Ontbijtkoek*? *Hutspot*? *Speculaas*? *Tompoes*? Can you help me find the original recipe for the delicious Dutch *appeltaart* my Oma used to make?

So you start making lists: of recipes sent and recipes requested. You search for Oma's famous *appeltaart*, for *bitterballen* that doesn't crumble and for genuine Asparagus Hollandaise. Somehow, overtime, you have tried and tested enough Dutch recipes for a proper cookbook. For all my readers and fans, scattered across the world, who shared their endless enthusiasm and hardy hunger for Dutch cuisine: this is for you! *Eet smakelijk* my friends, wherever you may be!

xo Colleen

Dutch cuisine

L et's be honest, the Dutch are not particularly well known for their cooking. It isn't often you hear people around the globe praising the Dutch for their upscale eats or gastronomical innovations. Do not be fooled, however; though often straight-forward and simple, Dutch food can be downright delicious.

From breakfast straight through to dessert, *Stuff Dutch People Eat* will lead you through a culinary adventure spanning flavours—and centuries!

 Starting your day à la Dutch is always a treat—whether you decide to top your toast with a sprinkly downpour or whip-up some traditional apple bacon pancakes, a Dutch breakfast is sure to bring out your inner child.

 Much has been said about the lack of creativity in Dutch lunch; however, don't despair—our recipes will add some zest to any *boterham*.

 Hearty dinner dishes such as the *stamppot*, *hutspot,* and *erwtensoep* may appear utilitarian on first glance, but they are sure to hit the spot and warm the soul on a blustery fall or winter's night.

 And who could forget all the delectable Dutch desserts? Whether you're craving an oeey-gooey *stroopwafel*, a celebratory *tompoes*, or a slice of the multi-layered Dutch-Indonesian *spekkoek*, we guarantee there's something for every sweet tooth!

Discover our 40 easy-to-make recipes that are sure to restore your faith in the delightfully delicious Dutch kitchen! *Eet smakelijk!*

The first Dutch cookbook

The first known Dutch language cookbook was printed in Brussels in 1514. The book, entitled *Een notabel boecxken van cokeryen*, 'A Notable Book of Cookery', contains over 175 recipes. The recipes are recorded in no particular order and include the likes of soups, sauces, meat dishes, fish dishes, savoury pies, tarts, and cakes. The recipes are said to come from various sources and origins—some can be traced back to Belgium and the Netherlands, although the vast majority stem from France.

During the 15th century it is said that Dutch cuisine was heavily influenced by northern French cuisine due to the country's proximity and the coinciding rule of the Dukes of Burgundy in both the Low Countries and Northern France. Recent research has found that 61 recipes in the *Notable Book of Cookery* were direct translations from a previously published French cookbook from 1490.

The cookbook gives a glimpse into European cooking of the 15th and 16th centuries. The often elaborate recipes identified the intended type of household, that of the very rich and affluent. Most recipes call for sugar (a luxury at the time!) as well as costly spices such as nutmeg, ginger, cinnamon, clove, and cardamon.

Scanning through the text is a fascinating read. Some recipes are obviously dated and bear witness to their

"Cover of Een notabel boecxken van cokeryen"

ancient time period such as 'Blackbird Pie', 'Pepper Sauce for Swans' and 'Harbour Porpoise'. Others like 'Venison Soup', 'Meat Pie', 'Almond Milk', and 'Boiled Lobster' would not appear out of place in a modern-day cookbook!

> Below are three **directly translated** recipes from the first Dutch cookbook *'Een notabel boecxken van cokeryen'*. We haven't tried these ourselves, so tell us how they turn out!

Om vleesch taerten te maken

To make meat tarts

Om vleesch taerten te maken Neemt daer toe vercken vleesch wten buycxken ghesneden ende welghesoden ende dan welghewreuen ontwee daer in herde eyeren ghesoden dye doren daer af wel tegadere gheminghelt ende cruyt Hier toe doet greyne/ ghiber/ caneel poeder/ noten muscaten/ groffels naghelen/ folie ende potsuycker alte ghader gheminghelt in dye spyse Ende dat salmen wel laten backen ghelyck eender pasteyen. maer het moet bouen open sijn ghelijck anderen taerten Alst ghebacken es stroytmen met caneele

(Direct translation): To make meat tarts. Take for this pork meat cut from the belly, well boiled and then well broken up [and] therein hard boiled eggs, the yolks of them, well mixed together and spices. Add to this grains of paradise, ginger, cinnamon powder, nutmegs, cloves, mace and pot sugar all mixed together in the dish. And one shall let it bake well, just like a pie. But it must be open on top just like other tarts. When it is baked one strews it with cinnamon.

Om soppen van amandelen

To make almond soup

Om soppen van amandelen Neemt vanden besten amandelen melcke dat ghi crigen cont Ende eest dat ghi wilt doet dair in rosinen Laet dat also dan te gader sieden tot dat dicke es Ende wilt men men mach daer toe nemen sofferaen daer layet een scoon verwe af Dit doetmen op die soppe ghelijck parey soppen. Dan stroyter men in dleste suycker op

(Direct translation): To make almond soup. Take the best almond milk that you can obtain. And if you want, put raisins in it. Let it boil thus together until it is thick. And if one wants, one may take thereto saffron; that lays a beautiful colour on it. One puts this over the soup just like parey soup. Then one strews sugar over it at the last moment.

Appel taerten
Apple tarts

Neemt appelen die alder best breken die suldy scellen ende wel cleyne sniden Maer wacht datter gheen carnen ofte sloechuysen in en vallen want die carnen souden dye gheheele taerten bederuen. Als dye appelen dus ghesneden sijn met cleynen stucken So suldi dien rant vander seluer taerten vullen tot boven toe al vol Dan suldi dair op maken eenen scheel vanden seluen deeghe daer die taerte af ghemaect es. Dan steltse inden houen ende laetse so backen alsse ghebacken is so suldise wt doen ende snidense bouen open inden scheel Soe dat die scheel maer en behouwe eenen ommerant. Dan suldise rueren met eenen houten lepel tot dat die appel wel ghebroken sijn die in de taerte ligghen Oft eest datmen wilt men machse duerdoen. Dan suldi nemen desen navulghende cruyden ende mingelense dair mede Te weten greine/ ghimber/ caneel/ noten muscaten/ groffels nagelen/ folie/ ende potsuycker Maer die dese selue taerte seer costelijck wilt maken die nemen daer toe moruwe suycker coecken ende ooc suycker daer men de coecken af maect Ende dit salmen temperen wel te gadere met sanen dan salment inde taerte doen mitten appelen ende latense also staen drooghen inden houen tot dat si drooghe es

(Direct translation): Take apples which are best for cooking until they fall apart. You shall peel these and cut them small. But watch that no seeds or pieces of core fall in, because the seeds would taint the whole tart. When the apples are cut up thus in small pieces, so you shall fill the crust of the same tart up to the top all full. Then you shall make a lid from the same dough that the tart is made from. Then put them in the oven and let them bake thus. When they are baked so, you shall take them out and cut a hole in the lid, so that the lid stays only as a ring around the edge. Then you shall stir with a wooden spoon until all the apples which lie in the tart are well broken up. Or if one wants, one may pass them through a sieve. Then one shall take these following spices and mix them therewith, to wit: grains of paradise, ginger, cinnamon, nutmegs, cloves, mace, and potsugar. But those who want to make this same tart very delicious take as well soft sugar cakes and also sugar which one uses for making cakes. And one shall stir this together with cream; then one shall put it in the tart with the apples and let it stand to dry in the oven until it is dry.

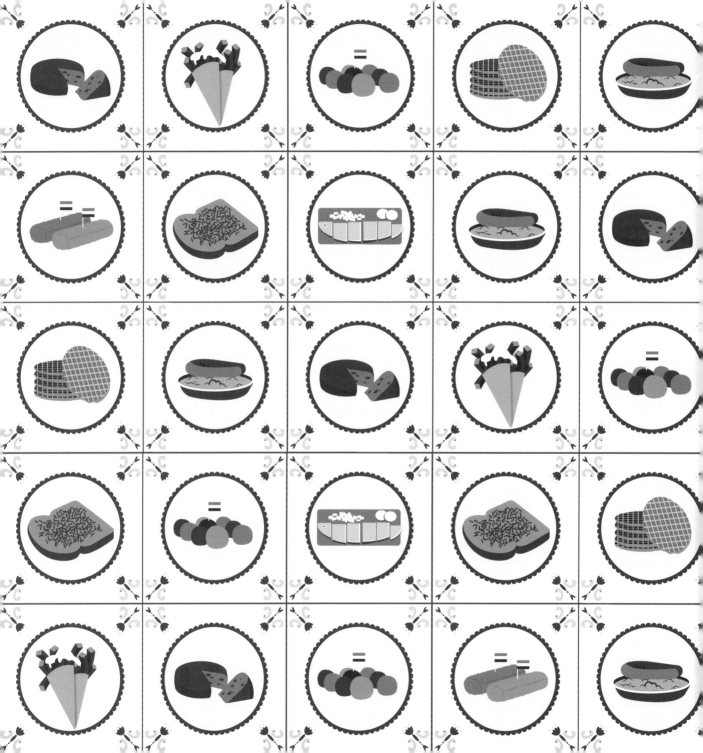

DUTCH
BREAKFAST

Dutch breakfast

The Dutch start their days with little fuss or fanfare. The Dutch breakfast is a rather practical, simple affair; no elaborate cooking skills, or time-consuming preparations required! There is, of course, a distinction between breakfast during the working-week or weekends, with the latter tending to be a bit more elaborate. For the most part, the Dutch breakfast—Monday through Friday—consists of bread, bread...and a little more bread! All jokes aside, bread and dairy do hold court at the Dutch breakfast table.

In a sense, Dutch breakfast and lunch do not differ so greatly; however, breakfast normally consists of bread with some sort of topping. Popular "topping" choices include the beloved *pindakaas* (peanut butter), Nutella, slices of cheese, *appelstroop* (a thick, sticky apple syrup), jam, or *hagelslag*.

Hagel-what?!

Of all the edible Dutch eccentricities, I would have to say that *hagelslag* tops the list. *Hagel* is the Dutch word for 'hail' and *slag* literally translates to the words, 'strike or blow'. When combined they evoke the connotation of a hail storm. *Hagelslag* is the Dutch answer to sprinkles. *Hagelslag* comes in several varieties (fruit-flavoured, white chocolate, milk-chocolate, etc.), but dark chocolate remains the staple. Interestingly, the Dutch take their dark chocolate *hagelslag* categorisation *very* seriously, as only sprinkles with a cacao percentage of 32% or more can officially call themselves *chocoladehagelslag*.

In most countries sprinkles are primarily reserved for children, topping the likes of cakes and ice creams. It is perfectly normal for Dutch adults to breakfast on thickly buttered slices of bread covered in chocolate sprinkles! *Yummm!* To put all this sprinkle-eating madness in perspective, it is said the Dutch consume over 14 million kilos of hagelslag each year—that's nearly a kilo per person!!!

Over the next few pages you will find several Dutch breakfast recipes. Most are 'weekend fare', but should you want to eat like the Dutch every day of the week, then get ready for a lot of bread... and perhaps a daily dose of chocolate 'hail'!

> **Funny Fact** The Flemish are said to aptly use the word *muizenstrontjes* (mouse-droppings) for *hagelslag*!

Wentelteefjes
French toast

Stuck with some not-so-fresh bread that you can't quite bring yourself to throw away? It's time to make *Wentelteefjes*! Commonly known as French toast—although it has many other names, like eggy bread and gypsy toast—*Wentelteefjes* is based upon a traditional Spanish Lenten and Holy Week recipe, but is now just as widely recognised as a breakfast staple as pancakes or waffles.

Methods for making *Wentelteefjes* can vary depending on preference, such as soaking the bread in juice or wine, but this recipe is the simple classic. And if you're wondering whether it would be better prepared with fresh bread instead, think again! Day-old bread is the best choice, as it won't fall apart when soaked with the egg mixture.

🍴 **8 slices**　🕐 **20 mins**

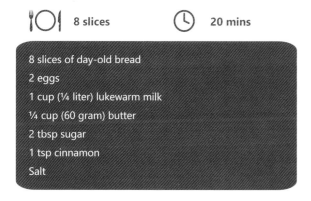

8 slices of day-old bread
2 eggs
1 cup (¼ liter) lukewarm milk
¼ cup (60 gram) butter
2 tbsp sugar
1 tsp cinnamon
Salt

 Use a larger flat bottomed bowl. Beat the eggs and stir in the milk, sugar, cinnamon and a pinch of salt.

 Cut the crusts of the bread and fully soak the slices in the mixture. Butter a frying pan and fry the wentelteefjes on both sides until golden brown.

 Serve hot with an extra sprinkle of sugar and cinnamon.

TIP　Tastes delicious with fresh fruit such as strawberries, blueberries or bananas!

Appel-spekpannenkoeken
Bacon & apple pancakes

If you often find yourself torn between a sweet or salty breakfast, then *Appel-Spekpannenkoeken* might be just the thing for you! *Pannenkoeken* are no ordinary pancakes—they're thinner and flatter than American flapjacks, but not as thin as French crêpes, and rather than being topped with extra ingredients, they're actually cooked right into the pancake! In fact, *Pannenkoeken* are more often eaten for dinner than for breakfast, and in the Netherlands and Belgium they're quite popular as the dish of choice for a child's birthday meal.

This bacon and apple version combines the succulent saltiness of crispy bacon with the subtle sweetness of fresh apples, pan-fried to golden perfection and drizzled with syrup.

serves 8   30 min

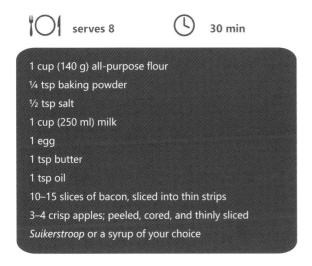

1 cup (140 g) all-purpose flour

¼ tsp baking powder

½ tsp salt

1 cup (250 ml) milk

1 egg

1 tsp butter

1 tsp oil

10–15 slices of bacon, sliced into thin strips

3–4 crisp apples; peeled, cored, and thinly sliced

Suikerstroop or a syrup of your choice

 In a large bowl, add the flour, baking powder, and salt, and mix thoroughly. In a separate bowl, whisk the eggs and the milk and mix into the dry mix gradually.

 In a large frying pan, add a few strips of bacon and a few slices of apple (distribute them evenly). You don't need extra butter since the bacon provides enough fat.

 Fry until bacon is slightly crisp. Then add enough batter to cover the entire bottom of the pan (spread the mixture evenly by tilting the pan). Flip the pannekoeken once when ready.

TIP   Serve hot, ideally with Dutch suikerstroop (a thick molasses-like syrup).

Ontbijtkoek
Spiced cake

Literally translated, *Ontbijtkoek* means "breakfast biscuit" or "breakfast cookie," although this spiced Dutch treat is actually a loaf or cake, and bears a striking resemblance to what is commonly known as gingerbread.

Ontbijtkoek has roots tracing back to Medieval times, which is evidenced by its use of such traditional ingredients as rye flour, honey, molasses, and a variety of fragrant spices. It is popular in the Netherlands as a breakfast bread, but is also widely enjoyed as a sweet treat at tea time. A thick slice of this richly spiced cake just wouldn't be complete without a generous spread of butter!

🍴 1 loaf   🕐 1 hr 10 min

1 cup rye flour

1 cup all-purpose flour

3 tsp baking powder

2 tsp cinnamon

½ tsp each of ground cardamom, ginger, coriander seed, and cloves

1 cup milk

½ cup brown sugar

½ cup honey

¼ cup molasses

¼ tsp salt

 Preheat oven to 160°C (320°F) and grease a 20-cm (8-in) cake tin.

 Thoroughly mix all of the ingredients together in a mixing bowl. Pour the batter into the prepared tin and bake for 60–80 min (test with skewer after about 45 min if center is cooked).

 Cool and serve in slices with a thick layer of butter.

Krentenbollen
Raisin buns

Freshly-baked rolls are a food staple for many cultures, and in the Netherlands, one well-loved variety is *Krentenbollen*. These fluffy buns can be slightly citrusy with the zest of orange and lemon, and are baked with raisins and currants for a touch of sweetness. Perfect for just about any occasion, a *krentenbol* works as a breakfast bun, a midday (or midnight) snack, a dinner accompaniment, a simple dessert, or even as a roll for sandwich-making if you like a little sweet with your savoury.

12 buns   **3 hrs**

3 cups all-purpose flour

1 cup currants

1 cup dark raisins

2 tsp active dry yeast

1 cup warm milk

2 Tbsp sugar

1 tsp salt

2 Tbsp unsalted butter, softened

1 large egg

½ tsp grated orange peel

½ tsp grated lemon peel

1 large cookie sheet lined with parchment or foil

1 egg whisked (to glaze)

 1 In a large bowl, mix the flour, salt, yeast, and milk. Add egg, sugar, butter, and citrus zests and stir thoroughly. Cover the bowl and let stand for 30 min.

 2 Knead the mixture into a soft, supple dough (you can knead by hand or by machine). Then add the raisins and currants into the soft dough. Place the dough in a greased bowl, cover it up and let stand in a warm spot for 45 min.

 3 Divide the dough into 12 equal portions and shape them into rolls, slightly flattened. Place on a baking sheet. Cover the rolls with a towel or oiled plastic wrap and allow them to rise until doubled, about 1 hr.

 4 Preheat the oven to 200°C (400°F). Brush the rolls with the beaten egg and bake them for about 15–20 min until done. Enjoy with fresh butter. Yum!

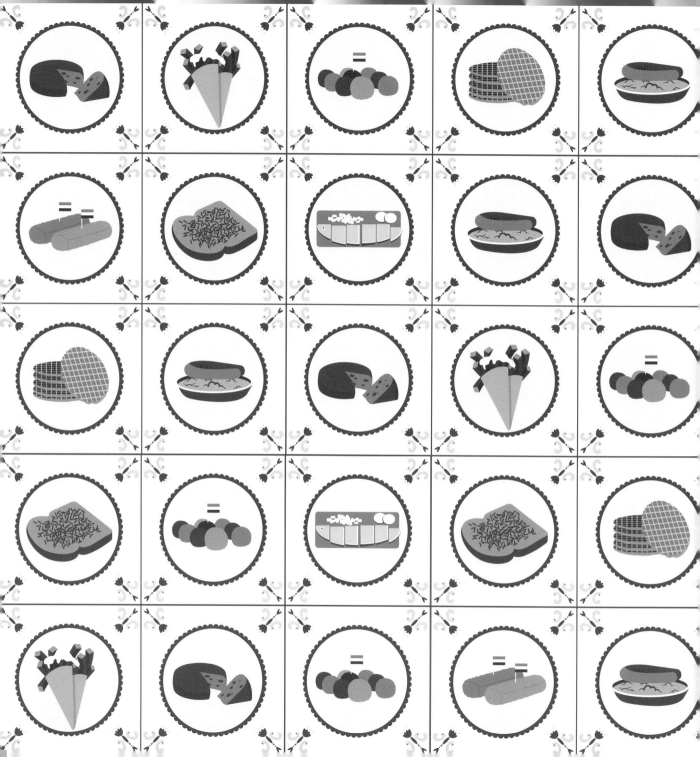

DUTCH
LUNCH

Dutch lunch

We're not gonna lie, the words "Dutch" and "lunch" have often led to disappointment. Step into any Dutch office cafeteria and you will find tiny boxes of *hagelslag* alongside endless rows of bread, cheese, and meat! When I first arrived in the Netherlands, I was shocked to see dozens of Dutchies eating the exact same lunch (of sliced bread) at the exact same time (12:30–1:00pm)! It shouldn't be a surprise then that the Dutch actually use the word *boterham* (literally "butter-ham") for sandwich, as often there is not a lot of creativity beyond the bread, butter, and meat.

Most Dutch workers lunch on rather utilitarian sandwiches with the vast majority of them brought from home. If you were under the assumption after visiting other European countries that the Dutch lunch in the same style as their French or Spanish neighbours, you couldn't be more wrong! Hot meals are a rarity, and long, jovial lunch breaks are certainly not the norm. An *uitsmijter* (bread with fried eggs and/or ham, cheese, and tomato) might be considered "spicing things up"!

Truth be told, the Dutch have greatly enhanced their lunches over the last few decades with the introduction of a multitude of jazzy sandwich spreads (aka *broodbeleg*). Some, though, are not for the faint of heart. You will definitely find your standard egg-salad or tuna-salad toppings, but the Dutch have also kicked it up a notch and made all sorts of new, slightly gooey concoctions. If you are feeling adventurous, why not try some *kipsatésalade* (blended chicken and peanut sauce), *en garnaalknoflooksalade* (blended shrimp and garlic), or *farmersalade* (blended farmer??). These toppings (minus the farmer!) all involve copious amounts of tasty Dutch mayonnaise. You may need to hop on your bike for a spot of post-lunch cycling to burn off those additional calories!

Over the next few pages, we'll dive into some hearty Dutch soups (great for lunch or dinner), a few of our favourite sandwich spreads, plus we will leave your mouth watering at the sight of some traditional Dutch snacks! *Broodje kroket*, anyone? Eat up!

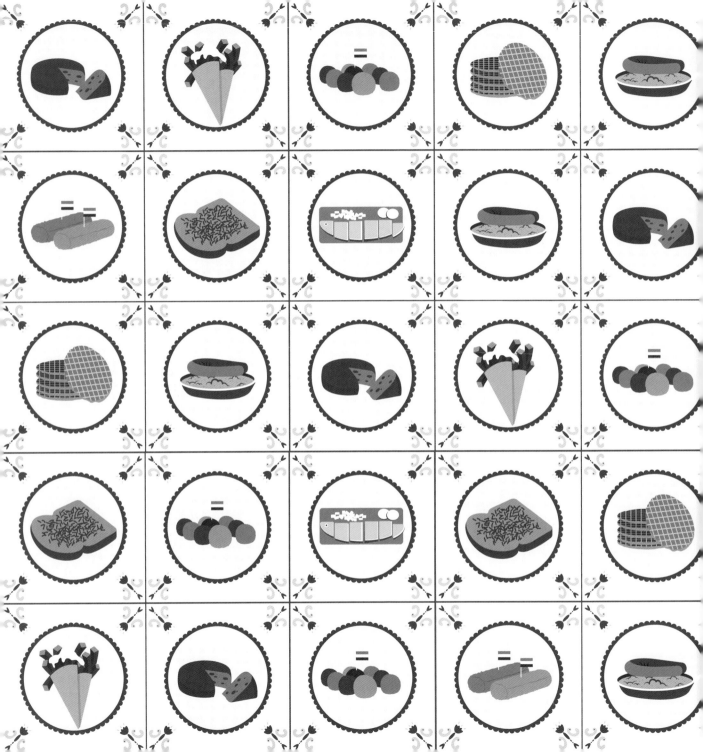

SANDWICH
SPREADS

Sandwich spreads

I have joked extensively in the past about the Dutch obsession with mashing, boiling, and deep-frying the heck out of their food! I could actually add a fourth culinary technique to the list: blending! It seems the Dutch have a persistent habit for developing new blended delights. Perhaps due to bread being ever present at the lunch table, you will observe great creativity when it comes to Dutch blended sandwich spreads.

You will literally find dozens and dozens of these sandwich spreads on the shelves of any Dutch grocery store, ranging from the traditional egg-salad to the *surimi-krabsalade* (Surinamese crab salad) and back. Of all the sandwich toppings and varieties, *Filet Americain* would be considered the most quintessentially Dutch! *Filet Americain* is the Dutch cousin of *steak tartare*, often in a pre-prepared grocery-shelf-ready way. It is essentially finely ground raw beef with added onions and seasoning. The first time I saw a colleague sit down with a piece of bread topped with *Filet Americain* I gasped, but now I will happily admit it is deliciously Dutch and has become of one of my favourites! (So much so that I spent much of my second pregnancy desperately craving the stuff!)

Now let's take a closer look at some tasty Dutch toppings and find out how to make a truly authentic *Filet Americain*—which in reality has little do with the good ol' US of A!

Kipkerriesalade
Chicken curry salad

When you're craving a curry but you also need a meal you can pack up easily for lunch, a quick *Kipkerriesalade* is just the thing. With only 3 ingredients, it's so easy to make, and quite versatile, too. You can mix it up with a freshly grilled chicken breast, but it's also a great way to use up any leftover cooked chicken from last night's dinner. And while this creamy and spiced chicken curry salad is usually served on bread as a sandwich, you can also spoon it on top of salad for a grain-free or lighter meal option.

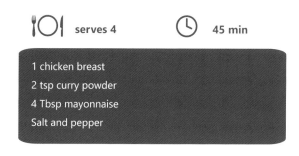

serves 4

45 min

 Poach or grill the chicken breast. Then leave to cool.

1 chicken breast
2 tsp curry powder
4 Tbsp mayonnaise
Salt and pepper

 Mix the curry powder with the mayonnaise and season to taste with salt and pepper.

 Shred the chicken or cut into small cubes and thoroughly mix with the sauce.

 Spread onto bread and serve immediately.

TIP   Add some chopped rucola to taste.

Eiersalade
Dutch egg salad

A timeless classic, egg salad has been around for hundreds of years, and its popularity does not appear to be waning anytime soon. While it was first served on salads, it's now most widely known as a sandwich filling, and it's hard to argue with this simple-yet-tasty, high-protein dish.

Great as lunch for one or to make in larger quantities for a picnic in the park, *eiersalade* is sure to be a hit among friends and family, especially with this slightly spruced-up version. In addition to the staple ingredients, this recipe also calls for mustard and chives, which add some extra tanginess and a fresh and peppery crunch.

🍴 **serves 4**   🕐 **25 min**

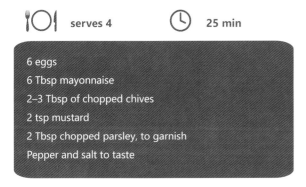

6 eggs

6 Tbsp mayonnaise

2–3 Tbsp of chopped chives

2 tsp mustard

2 Tbsp chopped parsley, to garnish

Pepper and salt to taste

 Boil the eggs for 7–8 min. Cool them off under cold running water and peel.

 Cut the eggs into tiny cubes and place in a large bowl. Add the mayonnaise, mustard, and chives and mix well. Add salt and pepper to taste and garnish with chopped parsley.

Filet americain
Dutch steak tartare

While ordering your steak rare is quite commonplace, and steak tartare (raw ground steak) is considered quite a delicacy, the Dutch have their own raw beef tradition called *filet americain*. This meat-lover's dream dish is made by mincing together high-quality sirloin steak with ingredients like capers, dill pickles, red onion, and mayonnaise. The creamy, savoury meat paste is then served on crackers or spread onto bread.

While perhaps not to everyone's taste, *filet americain* is certainly beloved by the Dutch, and because it's not widely known outside the Netherlands, is a dish that often inspires nostalgia and longing for those travelling or living abroad.

🍴 **serves 4**　🕐 **20 min**

1 lb sirloin steak

4 Tbsp Worcestershire sauce

1 Tbsp capers

½ tsp salt

½ tsp black ground pepper

4 medium-sized crunchy dill pickles

3 Tbsp diced red onion

3 Tbsp mayonnaise

2 Tbsp chopped parsley, to garnish

 Mince the meat in a food processor. Add all the other ingredients and grind to a nice paste.

 Serve the *filet americain* cold and raw on a nice slice of bread. Garnish with capers or fresh parsley.

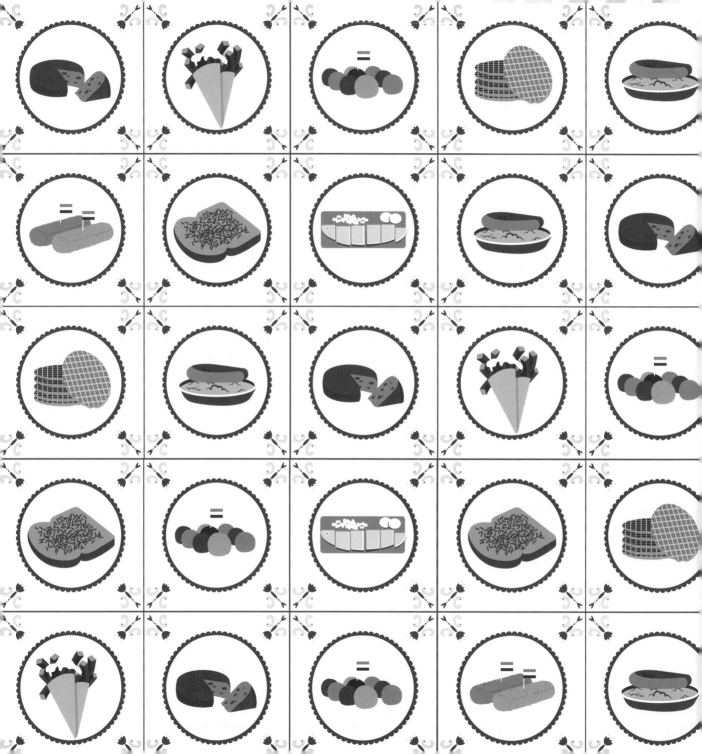

HERRING

Herring

The Dutch have a tremendous love affair with one particularly small, slippery, slimy, little fish: the hallowed Herring! The Dutch began fishing and trading herring over 1,000 years ago, and much of Holland's wealth and prolific history of sea trade can in fact be attributed to this tiny species. Business kicked into full swing in the 14th century when a Dutchman by the name of Williem Buekelszoon invented a tasty and popular process for curing the fish in brine.

For those brave enough to give the raw version a try, it's important to know that the very act of eating herring is an art form in itself. To truly "go Dutch," you must grab the fish by its tail, cock your head back to a slightly uncomfortable angle and take one large fishy bite. There's something about this delightful little performance that has even the most humble of Dutch persons brimming with pride.

Dutch people make a big hoopla about the kickoff of the herring season. Every year the seaside city of *Scheveningen* celebrates the opening of the season with *Vlaggetjesdag* (Flag Day) and the first barrel of herring is given to the King to sell at auction for charity. It's not unusual for the very first herring barrel of the year to sell for over €50,000!

How much do Dutch people really love their herring? Well, it turns out they consume over 12,000,000 kilos annually. That's at least five slippery delights per person each year! Of course this begs the question—have you met your quota!? If not, keep reading: we've got just the right recipe in store for you!

1E VAATJE

HOLLANDS
NIEUWE

2015

Haringsalade
Herring salad

Herring is quite the delicacy in European countries, and though it is often eaten pickled, traditional Dutch herring is salt cured instead, and makes for a lighter alternative to the many meat dishes found in Dutch cuisine. Herring is a great source of omega-3 fatty acids and is rich in Vitamin D and B12. *Haringsalade* (herring salad) is a particularly popular dish in the Netherlands during the holiday season.

In this dish, salt cured herring is combined with cooked beets and potatoes, capers, crisp apple, and crunchy onions and dill pickles, all mixed together with mayonnaise to create a creamy, tangy, and refreshing winter salad.

🍴 serves 2–3   🕐 40 min

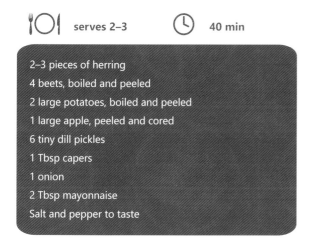

2–3 pieces of herring

4 beets, boiled and peeled

2 large potatoes, boiled and peeled

1 large apple, peeled and cored

6 tiny dill pickles

1 Tbsp capers

1 onion

2 Tbsp mayonnaise

Salt and pepper to taste

 Dice the beets, apple, and potato into small cubes and add to a bowl. Mix in chopped onion and dill pickles. Cut the herring into smaller pieces and add to the bowl.

 Add two Tbsp of mayo and mix carefully with the other ingredients. Continue mixing until the beets have coloured everything a purplish red.

 Add salt and pepper to taste.

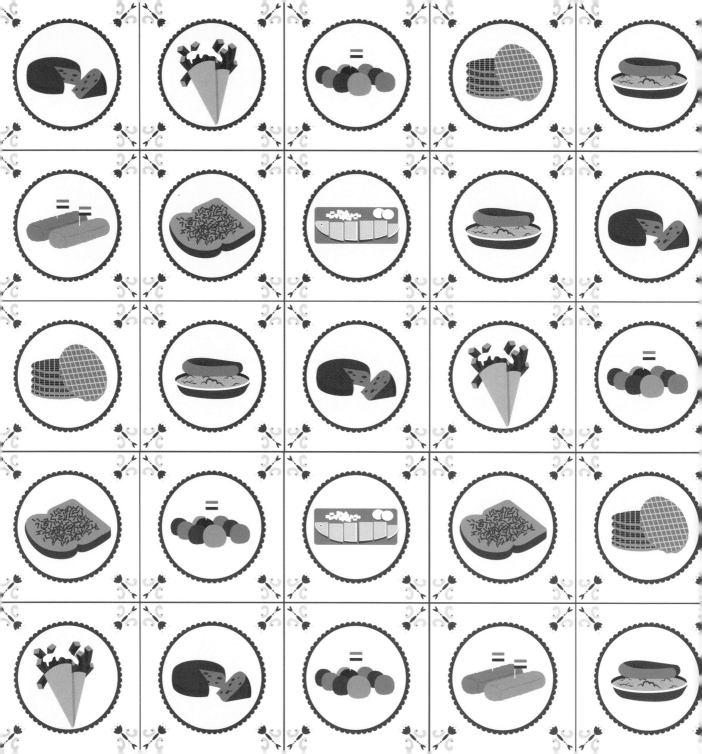

SOUPS

Erwtensoep
Dutch pea soup

Snert, snert, snnneerrrtt. The more you say it, the less likely you are to want to eat it. But trust me, although this short little word may sound inedible, its namesake is certainly not! Snert (also know as *Erwtensoep*)—is in fact, the Dutch word for traditional pea soup. This classic Dutch winter staple is a hearty meal in itself. There are endless variations on this dish and family recipes all tend to differ slightly. Some say the only true rule of thumb is to ensure 500g of split peas per litre of water. Others claim the soup is only a success if a spoon can stand fully upright on its own. One thing is for sure—you'll rarely find a Dutchie who doesn't have an opinion on what it really takes to make the perfect bowl.

Do you have your own winning recipe? Why not enter the Pea Soup World Cup? Think I'm joking, guess again!

 serves 4   1 hr 45 min

300 g (1.5 cups/10.5 oz) dried green split peas (if you use whole peas, you will have to soak them)

100 g (3.5 oz) thick-cut bacon

1 pork chop (5-6 oz/150 g)

1 stock cube (vegetable, pork, or chicken are all fine)

2 celery sticks

2–3 sliced carrots (½ cup/ 3.5 oz/ 100 g)

1 large potato, peeled and cubed

1 small onion, chopped

1 small leek, sliced (½ cup/ 3.5 oz/ 100 g)

100g celeriac, cubed (½ cup/ 3.5 oz/100 g)

Salt and pepper, to taste

Handful of chopped celery leaves

Handful of sliced smoked sausage, e.g. *Rookworst* (a Dutch smoked sausage) or frankfurter/wiener sausages

 Boil 3¾ pints of water (1.75 l) in a large soup pot, along with the split peas, stock cube, pork chop, and bacon. Skim off any froth forming on top as the pot starts to boil. Put the lid on the pot and leave to boil softly for 45 min, stirring occasionally.

 Carefully take the pork chop out, debone and thinly slice the meat. Set aside. Add the vegetables to the boiling broth and leave to cook for another 30 min, adding a little extra water every time the soup starts to catch. Add the smoked sausage for the last 15 min. When the vegetables are tender, remove the bacon and smoked sausage, slice thinly and set aside.

 If you prefer a smooth consistency, puree the soup with a hand-held blender until it is as chunky or smooth as you like. Season to taste. Add the meat back to the soup, setting some slices of rookworst aside. Serve split pea soup in bowls or soup plates, garnished with slices of smoked sausage and chopped celery leaf.

Tomatensoep
Tomato soup

"There's nothing quite like eating a bowl of tomato soup on a chilly, grey, or rainy day. It's warm and comforting, savoury and smooth, and probably brings back fond memories of childhood meals. But if you—like so many others—grew up eating tomato soup from a can, then this homemade version will bring you to whole new levels of comfort!

Full of bright flavours and fresh ingredients like tomatoes, onion, garlic, and Italian herbs, this recipe is also quick and simple to make, perfect for days when you're in a rush and just don't have the time to spend hours in the kitchen.

serves 4   30 min

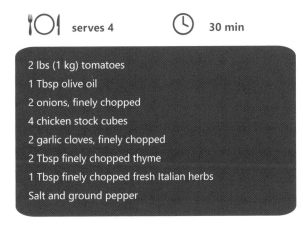

2 lbs (1 kg) tomatoes
1 Tbsp olive oil
2 onions, finely chopped
4 chicken stock cubes
2 garlic cloves, finely chopped
2 Tbsp finely chopped thyme
1 Tbsp finely chopped fresh Italian herbs
Salt and ground pepper

 Heat the oil in a large pan. Add the tomatoes (quartered), stock, onions, garlic, and thyme and bring to a boil. Let simmer for 20 min.

 Puree the soup in a blender (or with a hand blender). Season to taste with salt, pepper, and the fresh herbs.

TIP   Garnish with fresh parsley or a dollop of crème fraîche.

Aspergesoep
Asparagus soup

Asparagus is an extremely versatile vegetable. There are many ways to cook and serve it, and not only does it taste great, but it's also great for you! It's low in calories, but rich in vitamins and minerals, and in different cultures throughout history has been considered a delicacy and even an aphrodisiac.

Making this delicately delicious vegetable into a creamy soup is the perfect way to turn what is most often eaten as a side dish into a full meal. And if you have leftovers, you don't even need to reheat; it can be eaten cold as well as hot!

 serves 4–6   1 hr 15 min

2 Tbsp butter

1 onion, chopped

1½ to 2 lbs white asparagus, peeled and cut into 2-in pieces

6 cups chicken or vegetable broth

1 cup heavy cream

Salt and white pepper

2 Tbsp chopped parsley, to garnish

 Peel each asparagus stalk from the tip to the cut end. Chop off the tips and set them aside, then cut the stalks into 1-cm pieces.

 In a large soup pot, add the butter and melt it over medium heat. Add the onion and sauté until it begins to soften and melt, but not until brown since you want the soup to maintain a light, creamy shade.

 Add the chopped asparagus stalks and the stock and simmer until the stalks are very tender. This will take 20–30 min, depending on the thickness of the stalks. Pour everything into a food processor and blitz until very smooth, then pour the soup back into the saucepan.

 Bring the soup back to a simmer and add the reserved asparagus tips. Cook gently for about 5 min until the asparagus tips are just cooked through.

 Mix in the heavy cream over a very gentle heat, stirring constantly and taking care not to break up the asparagus tips.

 Finally, season with salt and pepper and serve the soup garnished with a sprinkling of parsley.

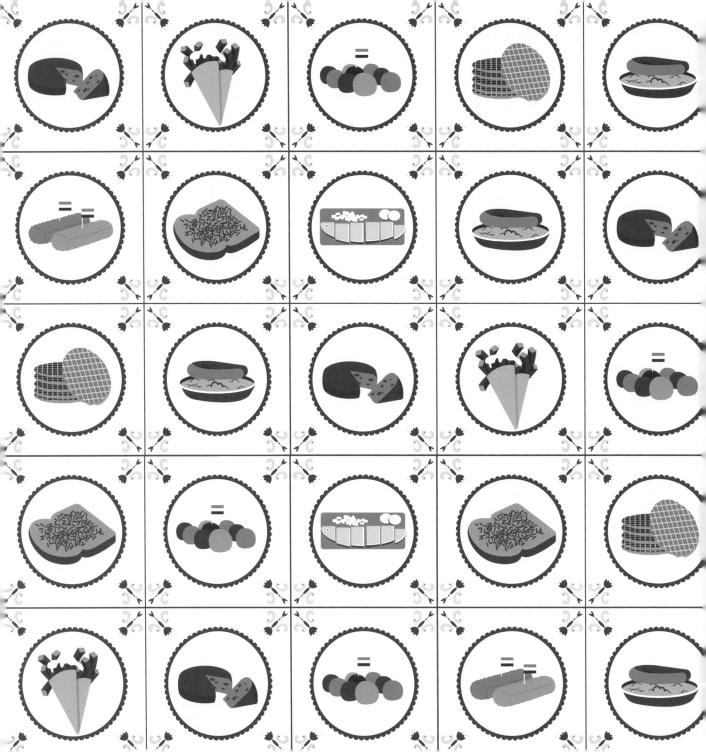

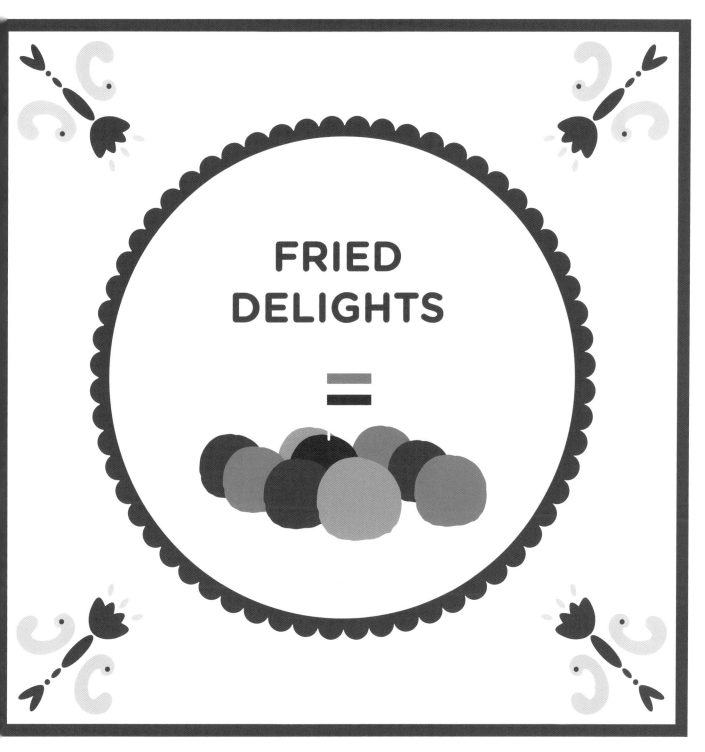

Fried delights

Some of the most popular Dutch delicacies are hearty and rich deep-fried delights, often sold at the neighbourhood snack bar or *patatkraam* (food truck), and also widely available as pub snacks in most drinking establishments. In fact, it's traditional in the Netherlands to enjoy a *bittergarnituur* (which literally translates to "garnish for bitters") while drinking alcohol. This platter of savoury food consists of a variety of tasty fried treats, although it can also include cheese and sliced meats. One item that will definitely be present, however, is *bitterballen*.

A beloved snack food in the Netherlands, *bitterballen* might look like meatballs, but are actually deep-fried balls of thick, creamy meat gravy. *Bitterballen* are the bite-size versions of *kroketten*, which are shaped into logs instead of being rolled into balls. *Kroketten* are so popular in the Netherlands that they can even be bought from vending machines!

Frikandel is another popular Dutch meat treat—a skinless, deep-fried sausage made from several kinds of minced-meat, and usually sliced down the middle to make room for toppings. Variations of this Dutch hot dog are also widely eaten in Germany, Denmark, and Belgium.

Another standard snack in Holland is *friet* or *patat*, which are Dutch-style fries. Although French fries may have originated in Belgium, the Dutch have found a way to make their own unique variation. In the Netherlands, *patat* is deep-fried twice for maximum crunch, but what really makes them stand out is the toppings. Sauces and condiments are the most important part of enjoying a paper cone filled with piping hot *patat*, whether you go simple and traditional with mayonnaise, or get a little more bold with curry ketchup, raw onions, or peanut satay sauce!

Bitterballen
Gravy-filled, deep-fried snacks

Have you ever tried to explain what a *bitterbal* is to a foreigner? It might, in fact, be more difficult than whipping up a fresh tray of the snacks themselves! A *bitterbal* is essentially a deep-fried crispy ball of meat gravy. It may sound a tad peculiar, but we guarantee they are worthy of a try!

Bitterballen are arguably the most popular of all snacks in the Netherlands and the perfect companion to a cold beverage. Nowadays *bitterballen* are most often eaten outside of the home. However, they are both easy to make and keep in the freezer, so we heartily suggest you add them to your Dutch cooking repertoire! A final note: *Bitterballen* are best served piping hot with a side of grainy Dutch mustard.

 serves 20   4 hrs

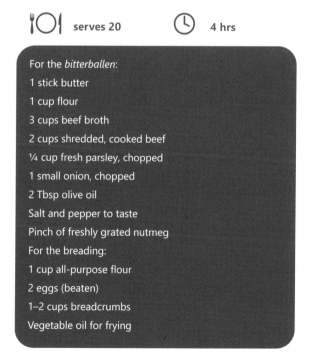

For the *bitterballen*:
1 stick butter
1 cup flour
3 cups beef broth
2 cups shredded, cooked beef
¼ cup fresh parsley, chopped
1 small onion, chopped
2 Tbsp olive oil
Salt and pepper to taste
Pinch of freshly grated nutmeg
For the breading:
1 cup all-purpose flour
2 eggs (beaten)
1–2 cups breadcrumbs
Vegetable oil for frying

1 Using a large saucepan, make a *roux* by melting the butter and gradually adding the flour until smooth. Slowly add the broth, making sure the *roux* is fully absorbing the liquid. Keep stirring until the *roux* thickens. Stir in the onions, parsley, and the beef and cook for a while longer until you have a nice thick gravy. Add salt, pepper, and nutmeg.

2 Pour the gravy into a shallow container, cover and refrigerate for several hours until the gravy is solid.

3 When the gravy is solidified, use a spoon and roll the thick gravy into small balls (3–4 cm diameter).

4 Roll the *bitterbal* lightly through the all-purpose flour, then the egg mixture, and finally the breadcrumbs. (Important: Make sure to fully cover each *bitterbal* in egg). Once you've breaded all the *bitterballen*, put them in the fridge.

5 In a saucepan, heat enough oil to fully cover the *bitterballen*. Fry them a few at a time until they are golden brown and then lay them on a plate covered in paper towels.

6 Serve the *bitterballen* hot!

TIP   Don't forget the mustard!

Kroket
Dutch-style croquette

The *kroket* is essentially the big brother of the Dutch *bitterbal*. *Kroketten* are often made from the same recipe as bitterballen, although they take on a larger oblong form, rather than a sphere.

The other main difference between the *bitterbal* and *kroket* is the way they are consumed. The *bitterbal* is a finger-food served with mustard and most often eaten as a snack alongside a beer or alcoholic beverage. The *kroket* is considered more of a meal. *"Broodje kroket"* refers to a *kroket* either served on a bun, or mashed up (by one's self) on a slice of bread. Step into any Dutch office canteen and you are sure to find more than a few folks enjoying a croquette sandwich of sorts.

Legend has it that the *kroket* was born from the minds of enterprising Dutch housewives in the 1950s as a handy way of converting leftovers from the night before into a quick and hearty meal. We're not sure of the legitimacy of this quaint story, but regardless of their origin, *kroketten* have remained a staple of Dutch cuisine for decades!

McDonald's in the Netherlands and Belgium actually serve a "McKroket," a *kroketburger* served on a bun with a mustard sauce. The McDonald's "McKroket" packaging reads *Wereldberoemd in Nederland* (World-famous in the Netherlands). If you say so!

Just use the same recipe for *bitterballen* to make yourself some nice *kroketten*!

Friet/patat
Dutch-style fries

Call them what you will—*friet, frieten, patat, Vlaamse frieten*—but one thing is for sure, the Dutch can't get enough of their crispy fried potatoes slices! How much do they love them, you ask? Well, enough to consume an astounding 41 million kilos per year!

In English we refer to them as French Fries, but unfortunately the French cannot stake claim this culinary invention. Sadly, neither can the Dutch. The birthplace of *friet* is said to be in Belgium, where stationed American WWI soldiers (mistakenly?) coined the term 'French Fries' in reference to the official language of the Belgian army at that time. Fries were commonplace in Belgium as early as 1680 but supposedly did not reach the Lowlands until the early 1900s. It is reported that the first *patat-friet* house popped up in Rotterdam's red light district in 1912!

 serves 2   1 hr 30 min

6 large baking potatoes, cut into strips

Oil for deep frying

Salt

Guide to Dutch toppings:

Friet met satésaus: fries with peanut sauce

Friet speciaal: fries with mayonnaise, (curry) ketchup and onions

Patatje Joppie: fries with the "top-secret" Joppiesaus (actually just a mixture of mayonnaise, ketchup and spices)

Patatje oorlog: this varies slightly by region but is often served as fries with peanut sauce, mayonnaise and raw chopped onions. Oorlog, the Dutch word for war, is a reference to the sloppy mess this dish entails

 Put potato slices into a large bowl and add salt. Fill the bowl with cold water and let soak for 1 hour or more at room temperature.

 Drain well and pat the potatoes dry with paper towels.

 Heat oil in deep fryer (or large pot) to about 325°F (165°C). Fry in small batches until lightly golden (about 2–3 min).

 Remove from the oil, drain on paper towels and set aside for a while.

 Then heat the oil to 375°F and fry again, in small batches, until the fries are golden (ca. 4–5 min). Drain on paper towels and sprinkle with salt.

Frikandel
Minced-meat hot dog

The *frikandel* is another über popular snack in the Netherlands which can be found in countless snack bars and lunch canteens scattered across the country. The *frikandel* is a hot dog or sausage of sorts, most often made from a combination of minced beef, chicken, and pork. What makes this Dutch dog unique is that unlike its American or German counterparts, it is first boiled and then deep-fried! The result is a crunchy texture that puts a tasty twist on the good ol' hot diggity dog!

serves 4–6   **1 hr**

1 lb (450 g) beef
1 lb (450 g) pork
1 lb (450 g) chicken
4 tsp salt
2 tsp black pepper
1 tsp ground nutmeg
4 tsp onion powder
1 cup whipping cream
Moulding options:
a) a professional sausage stuffing tool
b) a short PVC tube ca. 1–1.5 in diameter (3 cm)
c) a plastic bottle (cut off the bottom and stuff mass through)

 Add all ingredients to a food processor and blend thoroughly until you have a nice smooth mass.

 Use your moulding option of choice and create *frikandellen* of desired length.

 Bring water to boil in a large pot and cook the *frikandellen* for about 10 min.

 Let the *frikandellen* cool down in a fridge and then fry them in oil in a large frying pan (or in a professional fryer) for about 4 min.

TIP   Would you like to try *Frikandel* special? Cut the *Frikandel* down the middle , add raw onion, mayonnaise and curry ketchup (or regular ketchup). Enjoy!

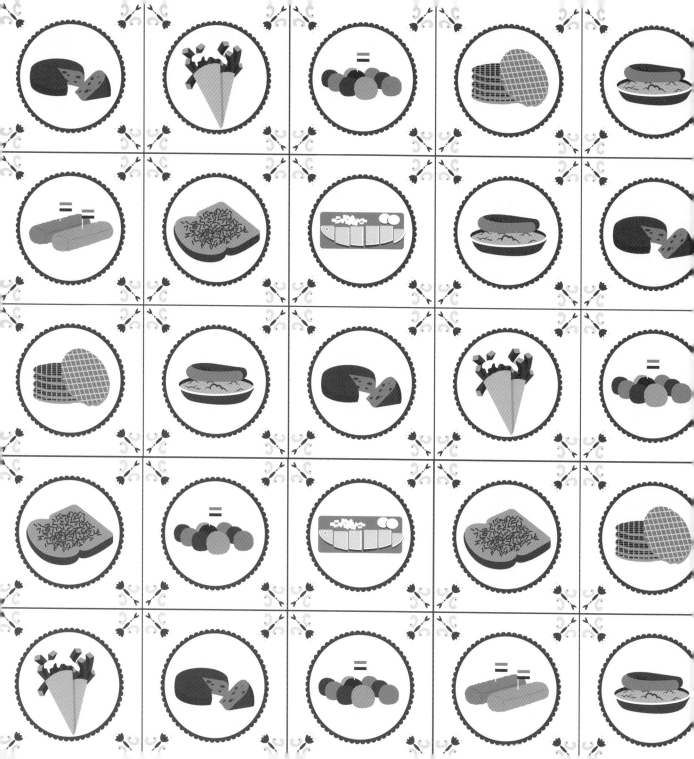

MAIN DISHES

"Kitchen Scene with the Parable of the Rich Man and Poor Lazarus",
Pieter Cornelisz. van Rijck, 1610–1620

Main dishes

The Netherlands has a wealth of delicious dishes that are rich in flavour and variety—not to mention history—many of them dating back to the Middle Ages. The traditional Dutch dinner is quite rustic and straightforward, usually a single-course meal consisting of vegetables, potatoes, and some kind of meat with gravy.

From the 17th to 19th century, Dutch labourers ate to replenish their energy after working long hours on farms or in unheated factories. Their cooking priorities were simplicity and nourishment, and though many of the traditional recipes have no doubt been altered and adapted since their original creation, even today, the essence of Dutch cooking remains the same as centuries past.

When it comes to dinner, many Dutch recipes feature slow-cooked meat combined with potatoes and various vegetables. *Draadjesvlees* (slow-braised beef) and *Hachee* (beef stew) are two traditional recipes not for the faint of heart or those short on time, as they require several hours to properly cook the meat (until it's so tender that it falls apart), but the results are well worth the effort.

A number of Dutch meat dishes call for aromatic spices—such as cinnamon, nutmeg, and cloves—to be used while cooking meat, in addition to the more traditional ingredients like butter, onions, and herbs. This combination creates a rich, fragrant mingling of sweet and savoury elements that gives Dutch meat dishes their unique and recognisable flavour.

Not all Dutch dinner dishes are beef-based, of course, nor are they all quite so rich and hearty as some of the more traditional recipes. The popular *Asperges met hollandaisesaus, ham en ei* is a much lighter meal featuring tender and delicate white asparagus and creamy Hollandaise sauce, which—though named after the Netherlands—is actually French in origin, part of the repertoire of classic haute cuisine sauces known as the "mother sauces."

Family Portrait, by Anonymous artist, 1627 (Rijksmuseum)

Draadjesvlees
Traditional slow-braised beef

Some good things just can't be rushed, and that's definitely true of *draadjesvlees*. This traditional Dutch slow-braised beef dish should not be undertaken by those looking for a quick meal, but if you have a couple of hours to kill, it's well worth the wait.

Stewing beef is slow-cooked with butter, onions, cinnamon, juniper berries, bay leaves, and cloves until it is so tender that it falls apart, and the combination of aromatic spices and seasonings gives it a warming savoury sweetness that sets it well apart from the usual pot roast.

🍽 **serves 4**   🕐 **4 hrs 20 mins**

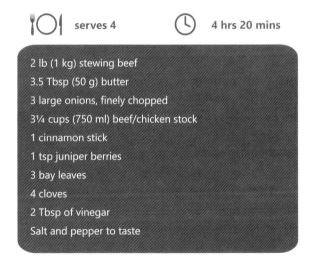

2 lb (1 kg) stewing beef

3.5 Tbsp (50 g) butter

3 large onions, finely chopped

3¼ cups (750 ml) beef/chicken stock

1 cinnamon stick

1 tsp juniper berries

3 bay leaves

4 cloves

2 Tbsp of vinegar

Salt and pepper to taste

 Cut the meat into medium-sized chunks. Melt the butter in a large pot (a Dutch oven is ideal) and brown the meat. Add chopped onions and sprinkle salt and pepper to taste.

 Add the stock, spices, and vinegar and bring to a boil. Once the stew comes to a boil, lower the temperature to the lowest level, cover the pot, and leave to simmer for at least 4 hrs.

 Make sure to check regularly and add more water if necessary. The stew is ready when the meat starts to fall apart. Remove the bay leaves, cinnamon stick, and any cloves and berries you can find. Serve with boiled or mashed potatoes and red cabbage. *Eet smakelijk*!

Gehaktballen
Dutch meatballs

There something about the taste of home-cooked meatballs that will always trump the store-bought variety, and that is definitely the case with *gehaktballen*. These Dutch meatballs are seasoned with parsley, coriander, nutmeg, and cinnamon—a combination that gives them a bold and unique flavour—and mixing the meat with milk-soaked bread will keep them juicy and tender when cooked.

Pair these *gehaktballen* with your favourite kind of potatoes and vegetables, slice them up and make a meatball sandwich, or simply eat them straight from the pan if you just can't wait. With meatballs this tasty, we really couldn't blame you for it!

serves 4   55 min

1½ lbs (680 g) ground beef

4 Tbsp butter

1 large onion, finely chopped

2 eggs

2 slices bread, finely diced

½ cup (15 g) finely chopped parsley

½ tsp ground coriander

½ tsp freshly grated nutmeg

½ tsp cinnamon

Salt & pepper to taste

1 Tbsp tomato paste

1 Tbsp mustard

½ cup beef/chicken stock

Milk

 In a large bowl, mix the meat with the egg, onion, salt, and spices. Soak the bread in a bit of milk. Press out the milk and add bread to the bowl. Mix thoroughly and form medium-sized meatballs.

 Heat the butter and brown the meatballs on all sides, turning them a couple of times.

 Lower the heat, cover the pan, and let simmer for a good 15 min, then turn them over and simmer for another 10 min. Add ½ cup of water to the pan, cover and simmer for another 10–15 min.

 Remove the meatballs, and add the stock, tomato paste, and mustard and bring to a high heat.

TIP   Some people coat the meatballs with breadcrumbs or flour before frying.
You can use ground beef or a mix of pork and beef.

Hachee
Dutch beef stew

Dutch beef stew is a perfect dish for autumn and winter, when the days start getting colder and we begin to crave foods that are rich, warm, and comforting.

Hachee dates back to the Middle Ages, when throwing together the last scraps of meat and vegetables was a good way to use up any leftovers and ensure that no food was wasted. Today it is a beloved enough dish in the Netherlands that it even has its own national day, so no meal-planning necessary on November 15th—just pull out your crock pot and cook up some *hachee!*

🍴 **serves 4–6**   🕐 **3 hrs 30 min**

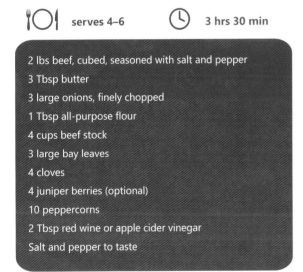

2 lbs beef, cubed, seasoned with salt and pepper

3 Tbsp butter

3 large onions, finely chopped

1 Tbsp all-purpose flour

4 cups beef stock

3 large bay leaves

4 cloves

4 juniper berries (optional)

10 peppercorns

2 Tbsp red wine or apple cider vinegar

Salt and pepper to taste

 The easiest way to make *hachee* is to use a slow cooker (e.g. Crock-Pot). You can add everything together in the morning, turn it on low and let it cook. When you return hours later, you'll be surprised to have a wonderful Dutch beef stew waiting for you!

 Alternatively, use a Dutch oven. Melt the butter over medium-high heat and brown the beef on all sides. Add the onions and some more butter as well as the beef stock. Sprinkle on the flour while stirring and mix in the bay leaves, cloves, and juniper berries.

 Finally, add the wine or vinegar. Bring to a slow boil, then lower the heat, cover the pot and let simmer for a good two hours.

TIP   Tastes delicious alongside mashed potatoes and red cabbage!

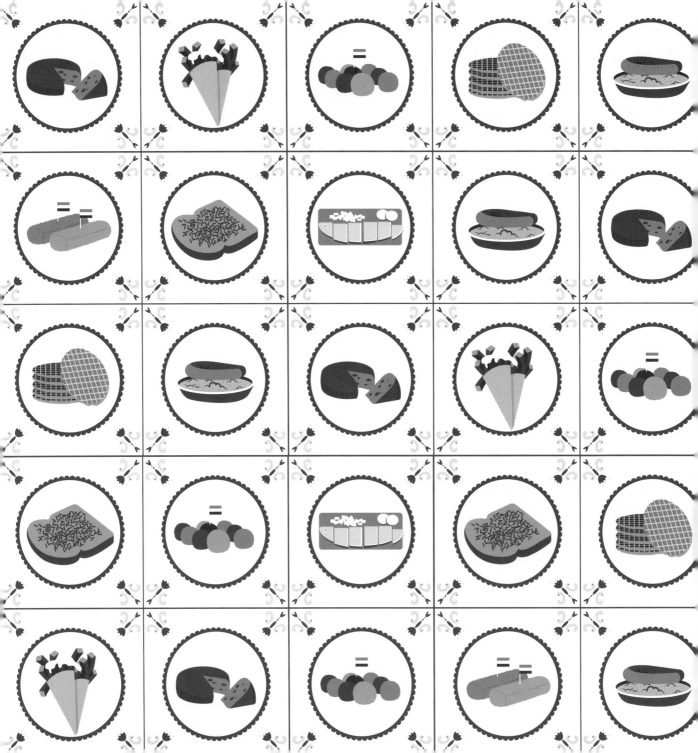

Mashing their food

I've joked about it before and I'll say it again: Dutch people have three very specific ways of preparing food and/or vegetables. They like to either:

> 1. mash the hell out of something
> 2. boil the shit out of something
> 3. deep-fry the life out of something

Let's discuss #1, the Dutch affinity for mashing! Based on Dutch cuisine, it appears that the Dutch love to mash, mash, and mash again! Case in point, the beloved *stamppot*. For those of you who are unaware of the *stamppot*, it actually combines two of the above Dutch cooking specialties: #1 (mashing) and #2 (boiling). First you boil the shit out of various veggies (potatoes, carrots, etc.). Then you mash the hell out of them, throw a little sausage on the side, and *voilà*, a perfect Dutch meal!

All kidding aside, the Dutch diet is a hearty one. It may not seem as refined as its French or Italian neighbours but it still knows how to please. You can, of course, find international cuisine anywhere in town, but nothing quite beats the traditional Dutch *stamppot* on a crisp winter's night. *Stamppot*, originating in the 1600s, is said to be one of the oldest of Dutch dishes. Yet for all its simplicity, it has managed to remain one of the country's most popular dishes. We'll show you that making your own *stamppot* isn't rocket science: it simply involves a lot of chopping, a lot of boiling, and a lot of mashing. Next time you're in the mood to feel like a Dutch farmer's wife (or the hired help for that matter), why not give it a try!

Hutspot met klapstuk
Potato carrot stamppot

A *hutspot* is a traditional Dutch dish made by cooking and mashing potatoes together with carrots and onions, which is then served with a side of meat. In this case, the *hutspot met klapstuk* combines this potato and vegetable mash with braised beef and gravy to create a meal that is similar to a beef stew, although different in preparation and presentation.

Because it uses such everyday ingredients, *hutspot met klapstuk* is the kind of meal you can make without having to go shopping for any hard-to-find foods, but the end result is still a delicious dish that will fill your tummy and satisfy your taste buds.

serves 4–6   2 hrs 20 mins

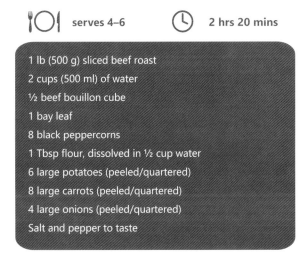

1 lb (500 g) sliced beef roast

2 cups (500 ml) of water

½ beef bouillon cube

1 bay leaf

8 black peppercorns

1 Tbsp flour, dissolved in ½ cup water

6 large potatoes (peeled/quartered)

8 large carrots (peeled/quartered)

4 large onions (peeled/quartered)

Salt and pepper to taste

 Using a Dutch oven or a braising pan, add water and dissolve the bouillon cube. Add the meat, the bay leaf, and the peppercorns and braise on low heat until beef is tender (1–2 hrs).

 Remove the beef, bay leaf, and peppercorns and mix the dissolved flour into the pan juices. Scrape the pot bottom and stir thoroughly. Increase the heat gradually until the gravy starts to thicken. Pour the gravy over the meat, set aside, and keep warm.

 Add the potatoes to the Dutch oven and fill with water, covering the potatoes. Add the salt. Next add the carrots on top and finally the onions. Cover the pot and bring to a boil, then lower the heat and boil for about 20 min (or until the potatoes are cooked). Remove the cooking water and set aside for later. Mash the potatoes, carrots, and onions thoroughly. Add cooking liquid if you require more liquids. Add salt and pepper to taste.

Hete bliksem
Potato apple stamppot

There are many versions of stamppot, and *hete bliksem* combines mashed potatoes and apples, with the addition of minced or chopped meat fried with butter and onions. After each component is cooked separately, they are mixed together and spiced with cinnamon (and perhaps a pinch of nutmeg!) to create a decadent dish of sweet and savoury flavours.

Hete bliksem, which literally means "hot lightning," is thought to be called such because the moisture in the cooked apples can retain its high heat so long that it burns the mouth of those eating it. In parts of Germany this dish is called *Himmel und Erde* (heaven and earth) in reference to its main ingredients—apples, which grow above ground on trees (heaven) and potatoes, which grow underground (earth).

serves 4–6   45 min

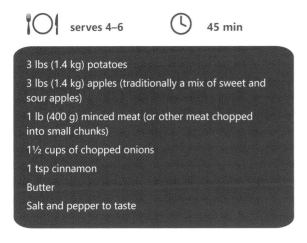

3 lbs (1.4 kg) potatoes

3 lbs (1.4 kg) apples (traditionally a mix of sweet and sour apples)

1 lb (400 g) minced meat (or other meat chopped into small chunks)

1½ cups of chopped onions

1 tsp cinnamon

Butter

Salt and pepper to taste

 Peel the potatoes, cut them into smaller pieces, and add them to a large pot. Add water so that the potatoes are just covered. Peel and core the apples, cut them into smaller slices, and add to the pot. Bring everything to a boil and then let simmer for about 20 min (or until potatoes are nice and soft).

 Add the chopped onions to a large pan and fry with butter. Add the (minced) meat and fry thoroughly.

 Mash the potato/apple mix to your liking of smoothness and add to the large pan with the onions and (minced) meat. Stir well. Add a tsp of cinnamon as well as salt and pepper to taste.

TIP   Add a bit of nutmeg for added flavour!

Boerenkool met worst
Kale stamppot

If you love mashed potatoes but struggle to eat your greens, *boerenkool met worst* is the perfect *stamppot* for you! In this traditional Dutch stamppot, potatoes are boiled and mashed into creamy green goodness with kale, milk, and butter, then served with slices of smoked sausage. This dish is a kale-lover's dream and a great way to add nutrient-rich leafy greens to a rich meat and potatoes meal. And even if you're not a big fan of kale, the combination of creamy mash and smoky sausage is sure to completely change your mind about these healthy greens.

🍴 **serves 4–6**   🕐 **50 min**

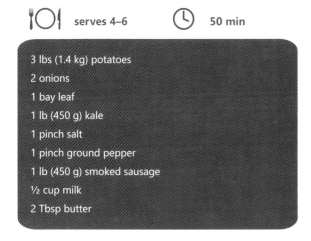

3 lbs (1.4 kg) potatoes

2 onions

1 bay leaf

1 lb (450 g) kale

1 pinch salt

1 pinch ground pepper

1 lb (450 g) smoked sausage

½ cup milk

2 Tbsp butter

 Peel potatoes and onions and cut into small pieces. Clean, trim, and slice kale.

 Add the potatoes, onion, kale, bay leaf, and a bit of salt into a large pan/pot. Pour in enough water to cover all. Put a lid on the pot and boil gently for about 20–30 min.

 Meanwhile, prick the sausage in several places and place in a skillet. Add enough water to completely cover the sausage and bring to a boil. Reduce heat to low and let simmer for 10 minutes.

 Discard the bay leaf, then drain the vegetables and mash them thoroughly. Add milk and butter and keep mashing until nice and smooth. Add salt and pepper to taste.

 Serve with slices of smoked sausage and enjoy!

Zuurkoolstamppot
Sauerkraut stamppot

Although its flavour is quite intense, sauerkraut boasts many nutritional benefits. Not only is it high in fiber and rich in vitamins, minerals, and enzymes, it also aids in digestion and—thanks to the fermentation process—actually becomes more nutrient-dense than raw or cooked cabbage once it's fermented.

Sauerkraut is the star component in *zuurkoolstamppot*, this traditional Dutch *stamppot* made with creamy mashed potatoes and mixed with crispy fried bacon and tangy sauerkraut. The bold and hearty flavours in this dish make it perfect comfort food on a cold winter's night.

serves 4   40 min

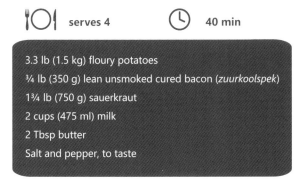

3.3 lb (1.5 kg) floury potatoes

¾ lb (350 g) lean unsmoked cured bacon (*zuurkoolspek*)

1¾ lb (750 g) sauerkraut

2 cups (475 ml) milk

2 Tbsp butter

Salt and pepper, to taste

 Peel and quarter the potatoes and then cook with salt for about 20 min. Meanwhile, cook the sauerkraut according to the instructions on the packaging.

 Melt half of the butter and fry the bacon.

 Drain the potatoes, pour in the milk, add the remaining butter, and grind to a smooth puree. Drain the sauerkraut and mix it along with the bacon into the mashed potatoes. Stir the stamppot on a low heat and add salt and pepper to taste

Andijviestamppot
Endive stamppot

Another popular *stamppot* is *andijviestamppot*, which is most commonly eaten in autumn and winter when endive is in season. This leafy green vegetable is similar to lettuce, and is mildly bitter with a slight nutty sweetness that pairs perfectly with creamy potato mash and the saltiness of smoked bacon and sausage. Unlike other *stamppotten*, the endive is not boiled with the potatoes, but is chopped and mixed in raw at the end, which gives the dish an added texture of crunchy freshness.

🍴 serves 4   🕐 40 min

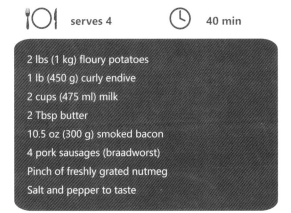

2 lbs (1 kg) floury potatoes
1 lb (450 g) curly endive
2 cups (475 ml) milk
2 Tbsp butter
10.5 oz (300 g) smoked bacon
4 pork sausages (braadworst)
Pinch of freshly grated nutmeg
Salt and pepper to taste

 Peel and quarter the potatoes and cook in a large pot of lightly salted water for about 20–25 min. Drain the potatoes and set aside.

 Meanwhile, fry the bacon until golden brown in a frying pan with some butter. Set aside. Fry the sausages in the same skillet until golden brown and cooked through.

 Add a dash of milk, nutmeg, salt and pepper, and three-quarters of the butter to the pot with potatoes. Mash the potatoes until they have the desired smoothness. Season with more butter, salt and pepper. Add more milk if the puree is too thick.

 Wash the endives and cut into small strips. Add handfuls of chopped endives and the bacon at a time while continuing to stir until fully mixed.

TIP   Serve the stamppot with the *braadworst* on top. Yum!

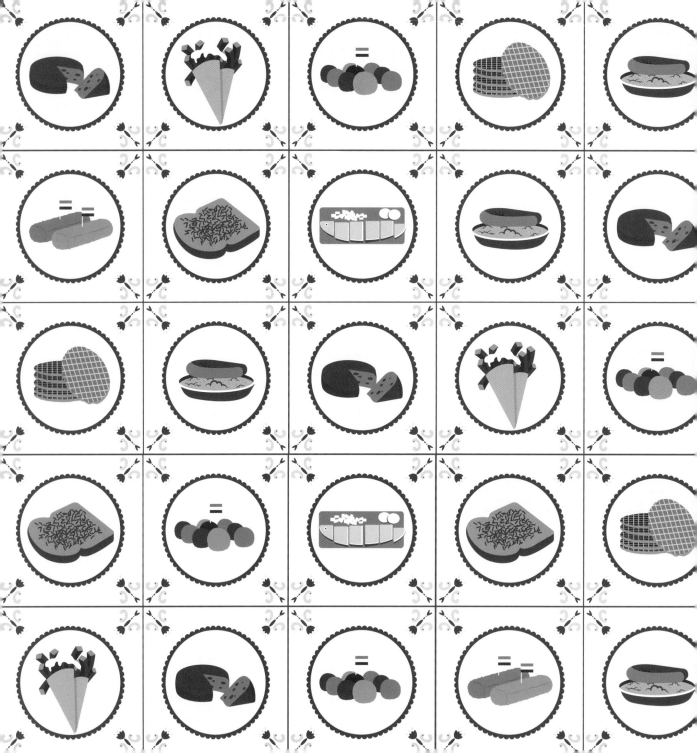

DAIRY

Dairy

The Dutch clearly have a long-standing love affair with dairy. Walk into any Dutch home, open the refrigerator, and you are certain to find a bounty of dairy-laden treats. Of course, milk, butter, yogurt, and cheese are staples in many homes around the world, but the Dutch differ in the sheer *quantity* of their consumption. Based on the latest data, the Dutch are the third-highest consumers of dairy in the world—beaten only by their Scandinavian neighbours, Finland and Sweden!

In my native homeland, Canada, we too have many a cow grazing on grassy fields, but drinking milk is a pastime mainly reserved for wee ones. I fondly remember sipping milk from the carton until the age of eight—but I believe that was the last time I drank a full glass of the white stuff. When I came to the Netherlands I gazed in shock, mouth wide open, at the rows and rows of fully-grown Dutchies sipping on their cartons of milk at lunchtime. Such a sight would never be seen elsewhere!

Is there a link between the Dutch's superior stature (i.e. the *tallest* people in the world) and their copious consumption of dairy? Some seem to think so. A unique study linked the number of cows per capita to the height of a country's people—and therefore it's no surprise the Dutch, literally, came out on top!

"The Milkmaid", by Johannes Vermeer, 1660

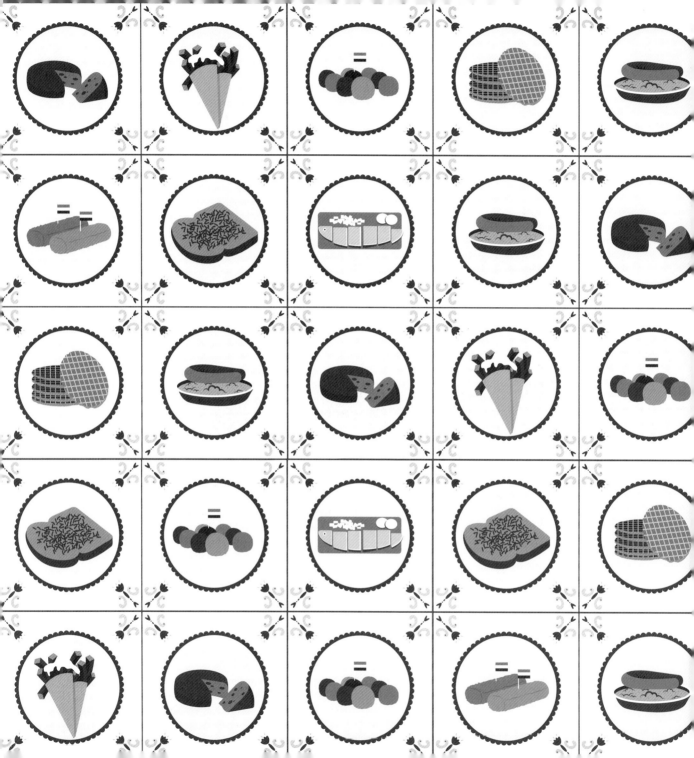

BAKED GOODS & DESSERTS

Stroopwafels
Dutch syrup waffles

Stroopwafels are one of the most popular Dutch desserts, and although these caramel-filled wafer cookies can easily be found in supermarkets, until you've tried them homemade you're sorely missing out. Like most baked goods, homemade *stroopwafels* far surpass the store-bought variety, so if you can get your hands on a waffle maker, this recipe is a must-try!

Literally translated, *stroopwafel* means "syrup waffle," which is quite an accurate description. The outside is made by baking dough in a waffle maker and thinly slicing it to form a wafer-like biscuit, which is then filled with sweet and sticky caramel syrup. The only danger in making these cookies at home is that once you try them you may end up eating the whole batch!

 makes 12 waffles **1 hr 30 min**

For the dough:

4 cups all-purpose flour

½ tsp ground cinnamon

½ cup granulated sugar

1 cup unsalted butter

2 large eggs

1 package active dry yeast (¼ ounce)

½ cup warm water

For the filling:

1½ cups brown sugar

1 cup unsalted butter

1 tsp ground cinnamon

6 Tbsp dark corn syrup

1 Tbsp vanilla extract

 In a kitchen mixer, add the flour, yeast, cinnamon, and sugar and cut in the butter. Gradually pour in the warm water and let the dough mix thoroughly. Then add the eggs one at a time. Lastly, add the pinch of salt and knead the dough well until it's nice and solid. Set aside to rise for 30–60 min.

 In a saucepan melt the sugar and the butter, stirring slowly over a low heat. Add the cinnamon and the syrup and continue to stir until the filling slowly bubbles. Keep stirring to avoid the mixture burning! Ensure all the sugar has dissolved completely and the caramel filling is nice and creamy. Finally, add the vanilla extract and mix it in. Keep the filling warm.

 Roll dough into 12 small balls. Squeeze each ball into the preheated pizzelle iron or waffle maker and bake for about 30–40 seconds (check instructions). Once the waffle is baked you will have to move quickly (otherwise the waffle will be too hard to cut). Cut the waffle in half and cover the bottom half with a generous amount of filling. Place the top half back on top and press gently to ensure the filling spreads evenly. Set aside to cool.

PRO TIP   Place a cold *stroopwafel* on a hot cup of coffee or tea and let it soften!

"The Waffle Baker" by Alexander Hugo Bakker Korff, c. 1850-82

Appeltaart
Dutch apple pie

Nothing says autumn quite like a freshly baked apple pie, and *appeltaart* is one of those classic desserts that never goes out of style. Tart, juicy apple filling inside a golden, flaky pastry shell; the main elements of a delicious apple pie are the same worldwide, but this Dutch version has a few unique elements that help it stand out in the crowd.

Recipes for *appeltaart* have been traced back to the Middle Ages, but today there are two popular varieties of traditional Dutch apple pie: one with a crumb topping and one topped with dough laid in a lattice pattern. In both styles, cinnamon, lemon juice, and raisins are added to the apple filling, which gives the pie a more complex flavour profile and an extra citrus zest.

 serves 6   2 hrs 15 min

11 oz (300 g) self-rising flour

7 oz (200 g) butter

5 oz (150 g) light brown sugar

¾ egg for the dough

¼ beaten egg for brushing

Pinch of salt

2 lbs (1 kg) apples

Fresh lemon juice

2 tsp ground cinnamon

¼ cup (50 g) sugar

⅓ cup (50 g) dry raisins (optional)

 1. Mix flour, salt, brown sugar, and butter in cubes. Add the ¾ egg and nicely knead the ingredients into a smooth dough. Leave to rest in the fridge for an hour.

 2. Peel the apples and cut into thick slices. Add the slices into a separate bowl and sprinkle with lemon juice, cinnamon, and sugar and stir. Add the raisins (optional). Cover and set aside.

 3. Preheat the oven to 175ºC (350ºF). Line a round buttered baking tin (20–22 cm) with 60% of the dough. Add the prepared apples and distribute the slices evenly.

 4. With the leftover 40% of the dough, make a grid on top of the apples. In a small bowl, add the ¼ egg and a bit of water and stir. Brush the grid lightly with the egg mixture. Bake the pie for about 60–70 min.

 5. Serve warm or cold with whipped cream or a scoop of vanilla ice cream!

Tompoes
Dutch mille-feuille pastry

This custard-filled puff pastry slice, called *tompoes*, or *tompouce* (a reference to "Tom Thumb"), is a beloved dessert in the Netherlands, popularly served with tea or coffee at celebratory events. Funnily enough, *tompoes* are also a common dessert when meeting or visiting the in-laws for the first time. Though tasty, *tompoes* are notoriously difficult to eat without making a mess, as the pastry is so brittle and flaky, so making a good impression while eating one of these custard slices is a nearly impossible feat!

serves 8   **45 min**

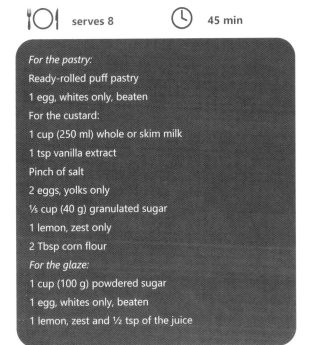

For the pastry:
Ready-rolled puff pastry
1 egg, whites only, beaten
For the custard:
1 cup (250 ml) whole or skim milk
1 tsp vanilla extract
Pinch of salt
2 eggs, yolks only
⅛ cup (40 g) granulated sugar
1 lemon, zest only
2 Tbsp corn flour
For the glaze:
1 cup (100 g) powdered sugar
1 egg, whites only, beaten
1 lemon, zest and ½ tsp of the juice

 For the pastry: Preheat the oven to 400°F (205°C). Spray a baking sheet with cooking spray. Cut the puff pastry into rectangular pieces (typical *tompoes* are ca. 2.5 in x 5 in or 6 cm x 12 cm). Place pastry rectangles on the baking sheet and brush with egg. Bake for 10-15 min or until the pastry turns golden brown.

 For the custard: In a bowl, beat the egg yolks, then add sugar and the lemon zest and whisk until light and foamy. Add the corn flour and a few Tbsp of warm milk and whisk to prevent lumps.

 In a saucepan, heat the milk with the vanilla and salt over a low heat. Add the egg mixture and whisk continuously until the custard is nice and thick. Remove from the heat and press some plastic wrap onto the surface of the custard to prevent a skin from forming.

 For the glaze: Combine the powdered sugar, lemon juice, egg white, and zest. Whisk for about five min.

 Making the *tompoes*: Hold the hot pastry in a kitchen towel and carefully slice each rectangle into 2 layers with a sharp knife (be careful not to burn yourself!). Take the bottom part of a baked pastry and spread the cooled custard on it. Place the other pastry half on top and glaze thoroughly.

Stoofpeertjes
Dutch stewed pears

Stoofpeertjes, or stewed pears, are unique in that they can just as easily be served as a side dish alongside a savoury dinner as they can be eaten on their own for dessert (topped with a dollop of ice cream, of course!). This dish is quite simple to make, as long as you've got time to let the pears simmer, but the result is well worth the wait—soft, juicy pears saturated with red wine and blackcurrant liqueur and spiced with cloves and cinnamon. It's a sweet and fragrant dessert that is rich in flavour while maintaining a light and fruity freshness.

serves 4   2 hrs 45 min

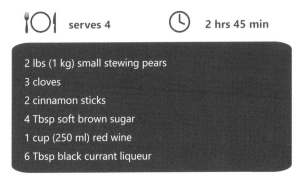

2 lbs (1 kg) small stewing pears

3 cloves

2 cinnamon sticks

4 Tbsp soft brown sugar

1 cup (250 ml) red wine

6 Tbsp black currant liqueur

 1 Peel the pears and leave whole with stems intact.

 2 Stick the cloves into the lemon rind. Put the pears, cinnamon sticks, and sugar in a large pan and pour in the red wine and liqueur. Add enough water to just cover the pears.

3 Bring to the boil and leave the pears to simmer, covered, for 2.5 hrs until tender.

 4 Lift the pears carefully out of the pan, serve on a plate with some cinnamon ice cream and whipped cream.

Limburgse kersenvlaai
Limburger cherry pie

The region of Limburg in the Netherlands is so famous for its pies that these Dutch desserts are named for it. *Limburgse vlaaien* (Limburger pies)—often simply referred to as *vlaaien*—are most often made for special occasions, such as birthdays or funerals. Though *vlaais* look similar to traditional pies, the pastry is made using yeast dough with very little butter, unlike the shortcrust pastry used for most pies and tarts. *Limburgse Kersenvlaai* uses juicy and plump cherries for a *vlaai* that's sure to satisfy your sweet tooth!

🍴 serves 6   🕐 2 hrs

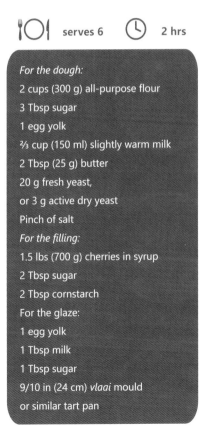

For the dough:

2 cups (300 g) all-purpose flour

3 Tbsp sugar

1 egg yolk

⅔ cup (150 ml) slightly warm milk

2 Tbsp (25 g) butter

20 g fresh yeast,
or 3 g active dry yeast

Pinch of salt

For the filling:

1.5 lbs (700 g) cherries in syrup

2 Tbsp sugar

2 Tbsp cornstarch

For the glaze:

1 egg yolk

1 Tbsp milk

1 Tbsp sugar

9/10 in (24 cm) *vlaai* mould
or similar tart pan

 Dissolve the yeast and sugar in milk and let stand for 10–15 min. In a large bowl, add flour, salt, and sugar and combine. Now add the milk and egg and stir it together. Finally, add the soft butter. Knead for 5–10 min with an electric mixer or for 10–15 min by hand. The dough should be smooth and elastic. Put the dough in a greased bowl, cover and let it rest for 1–1.5 hrs in a warm place (the dough should roughly double in volume).

 For the filling, drain the cherries and put the syrup in a saucepan over medium heat. In a small bowl, combine 4 Tbsp of the syrup with cornstarch and whisk well until completely dissolved. Pour the cornstarch mixture and sugar into the hot cherry syrup and mix well. Cook over a low heat and stir frequently until the mixture is nice and thick. Remove from the heat and add cherries. Set aside and let cool completely.

 Preheat the oven to 430°F (220°C). Prepare a 9/10 in (24cm) *vlaai* mould or similar tart pan by greasing it with butter or spraying it with some oil. Take about ⅔ of the dough and roll it into a nice circle, about 0.12 in (3mm) thick. Leave the excess dough hanging over the edges, but make sure the dough inside the mould is neatly fitted. Cover it and let it sit for about 10 min.

 Now with a rolling pin, trim off the edges/excess dough by carefully pressing it along the rim of the mould. Add the cherry pie filling and distribute evenly. Roll out the remaining dough and cut it into strips of about 0.5 in (1.5 cm) wide. Place the strips over the filling to create a crisscross lattice pattern.

 Brush the lattice with egg wash (a yolk lightly beaten with 1 Tbsp of milk) and sprinkle with brown sugar. Put the vlaai in the oven and bake for about 25–30 min.

 Remove from the oven, place on a wire rack and leave to cool for 20 min, then remove the pie from the tin and let it cool completely. Serve with a dollop of whipped cream!

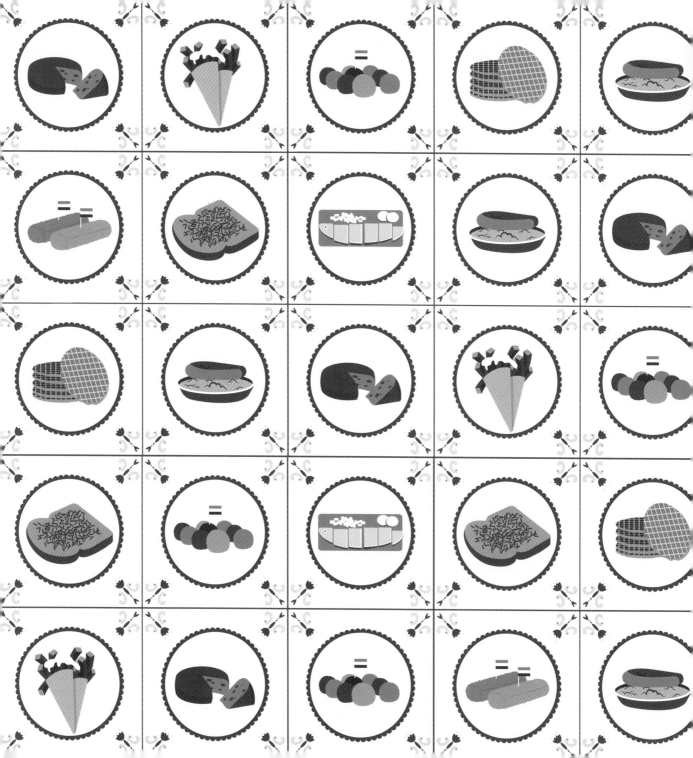

SINTERKLAAS

"The feast of St. Nicholas" Jan Steen 1663–1665

Sinterklaas

Sinterklaas is the most beloved of all Dutch holidays and traditions. And one that Dutch people are fiercely proud of. The modern-day figure of Santa Claus is actually derived from the Dutch *Sinterklaas* figure who was named after St. Nicholas, a bishop living in 3rd-century Turkey.

The holiday season in the Netherlands officially starts in mid-November, with the arrival of *Sinterklaas* and his legion of helpers (*Zwarte Piet*). *Sint* arrives by steamboat from Spain, where he is said to live year-round, and parades through town on his white horse to the glee of Dutch children everywhere. Celebrated on the fifth of December, *Sinterklaasavond* (*Sinterklaas* night) or *Pakjesavond* (present night) is a family affair featuring festive food, treats, gift-giving, and poems.

The celebration of *Sinterklaas* in the Netherlands has taken place for centuries. Jan Steen, the quintessential Dutch *Golden Age* painter, captured the festive occasion in his 1665 painting entitled, "*Het Sint Nicolaasfeest*" (The Feast of Saint Nicholas). The painting, now hung in Amsterdam's Rijksmuseum, portrays a Dutch family celebrating *Sinterklaas* in their family home on the night of December 5th. This centuries-old scene could still easily depict modern day celebrations: a "nice" daughter unpacking toys from a shoe, with a "naughty" older brother in tears at the sight of his empty shoe. A third brother looks on, laughing, as the rest of the family inspect the nearby chimney for traces of *Sint's* entrance. Most notable, the painting includes a multitude of baked treats—*kruidnoten*, waffles, *duivekater*, *taai-taai* and *speculaas*—which are all still very much a part of today's *Sinterklaas* traditions!

From *pepernoten*, *speculaas* to chocolate letters, *Sinterklaas* and the holiday season in the Netherlands abounds with—uniquely Dutch—sweet treats. Don't let their long-standing history scare you off; their recipes are, in fact, *a piece of cake!*

Pepernoten
Mini spiced cookies

You say *kruidnoten*, I say *pepernoten*? There appears to some confusion in the Netherlands as to which cookie is actually which. Dutch bakers often make a distinction between *pepernoten* and *kruidnoten*; however, most people nowadays refer to the small, round cookies associated with *Sinterklaas* as *pepernoten*, so we will too! Looking to celebrate *Sinterklaas* in true Dutch fashion? Whip up a batch of these deliciously spiced cookies to mark the start of the festive season—and watch the children scramble!

🍴 Ca. 50 *pepernoten*   🕐 50 min

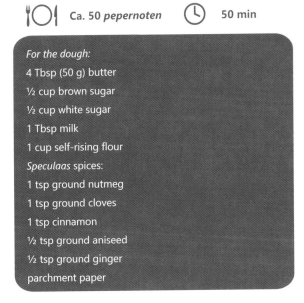

For the dough:
4 Tbsp (50 g) butter
½ cup brown sugar
½ cup white sugar
1 Tbsp milk
1 cup self-rising flour
Speculaas spices:
1 tsp ground nutmeg
1 tsp ground cloves
1 tsp cinnamon
½ tsp ground aniseed
½ tsp ground ginger
parchment paper

 In a large bowl, cream the butter and sugar, then add the spices. Add the flour and milk, and knead everything together into a stiff dough. Add a Tbsp or more of water if needed. Rest the dough in the fridge for a couple of hours so the flavors can properly blend (optional for optimal taste!).

 Roll small marble-sized balls and place them on parchment paper on a baking sheet. Press the balls slightly to give them the characteristic shape of *pepernoten*.

 Bake at 400°F (205°C) for about 10–15 min until nicely browned.

Speculaas
Dutch spiced cookies

When it comes to holiday baking, *speculaas* are a must-have in any Dutch kitchen. Traditionally made for the feast of St. Nicholas on December 5th, these thin, crunchy, spiced biscuits have gained popularity worldwide as a much-loved Christmas cookie.

Speculaas are easily recognisable in appearance as well as by taste. The combination of spices like cinnamon, nutmeg, and cloves gives them a distinctively festive flavour, and the name of these cookies, taken from the Latin word *speculum* (meaning "mirror"), references the design or image that is traditionally imprinted on the top of each cookie using a wooden mold. And the most common design? Why, a windmill, of course!

🍴 **serves 24**   🕐 **45 min**

3 cups flour

1½ cups brown sugar

1 cup butter

1 egg

2 Tbsp milk

1 tsp baking powder

1½ tsp ground cinnamon

¼ tsp salt

½ tsp ground nutmeg

½ tsp ground cloves

½ cup chopped blanched almonds (optional)

 1) In a bowl, soften the butter and then gradually add and combine the remaining ingredients. Knead thoroughly until fully mixed.

 2) Place the dough in the fridge and let rest for a few hours. This will give the spices and other ingredients more time to properly blend (optional).

 3) Divide dough in half.

 4) On a lightly floured surface, roll one portion of the dough to ⅛-in (3 mm) thickness. Cut into desired shapes, place on greased cookie sheet and decorate with almonds (optional). If you want to use traditional wooden moulds, then it is important to rub the inside thoroughly with flour (this will make it easier for the cookies to come out afterwards).

 5) Repeat with second half of dough. Bake at 350°F (180°C) for 10–15 min, or until browned.

 6) Remove and allow to cool.

Gevulde speculaas
Filled spice cake

Another traditional Christmas dessert in the Netherlands is *gevulde speculaas*, a spiced cake filled with homemade *amandelspijs* (almond paste) and topped with almonds. Its rich and heady flavour comes from the *speculaas* spices, a blend of aromatic spices—cloves, nutmeg, ginger, cinnamon, and cardamom—imported from Indonesia during the Dutch East Indies spice trade in the 17th century, a combination which is still used in many Dutch baking recipes today.

serves 6   2 hrs 40 min

For the almond paste:
1 cup (125 g) raw blanched almonds
½ cup (125 g)) granulated sugar
1 large egg
1 tsp lemon zest
1 Tbsp almond flavouring
For the dough:
1½ cups (250 g) all-purpose flour
1 cup (150 g) brown sugar
¾ cup (175 g) unsalted butter
1 tsp baking powder
Pinch of salt
For the speculaas spices:
1 tsp ground cloves
½ tsp nutmeg
1 tsp ginger
1 tsp cardamom
1 tsp coriander
1 tsp anise
For baking:
Whole almonds without skins
for decoration
1 large egg

 For the almond paste: Add the almonds, sugar, almond flavouring, and zest to a food processor and grind for a few min until very fine. Add the egg and grind further until you have a fine paste. Store in fridge.

 For the dough: In a large bowl, add the flour, baking powder, sugar, salt, and spices and mix thoroughly. Soften the butter and add it to the dry ingredients. Knead until you get a smooth dough. Add a bit of milk if necessary. Wrap dough in foil and put in the refrigerator for a few hrs (the longer you let the dough rest, the better as the spices will blend further).

 For Baking: Preheat oven to 350°F (180°C). Grease a shallow baking pan 8×10 in (20×26 cm) or round with a diameter of 10 in (26 cm). Divide the dough into two parts and roll out both portions on a lightly floured surface until they are roughly the size of the baking pan.

 Place one of the layers in the pan, pressing it lightly to ensure it fills the entire pan. Lightly beat the egg with a tsp of cold water and brush ⅓ of the egg mix over the dough layer in the pan.

 Roll out the almond paste until it is the size of the pan. Gently place it over the dough in the pan and press the paste lightly down. Brush the next ⅓ of the egg over it.

 Place the second layer of dough on top of the paste, press lightly, and make as smooth as possible. Brush the last ⅓ of the egg over the dough.

 Decorate the pastry with the almonds. Use traditional patterns or be creative!

 Put the pan in the oven and bake for 40 min. Let cool completely in the pan, then cut it in portions as you like.

Banketstaaf
Almond-paste-filled pastry log

Holiday season in the Netherlands just wouldn't be complete without *banketstaaf*, a log-shaped puff pastry filled with almond paste. And while these festive treats are sure to be found in every Dutch bakery as Christmastime approaches, why not skip the queues and bake your own at home? It's a no-fail recipe if you use good quality puff pastry, and making the almond paste (*amandelspijs*) from scratch is really quite straightforward. With only two components, the pastry and the *amandelspijs*, *banketstaaf* is a perfect example of deliciousness found in even the simplest of recipes.

serves 2 logs   **40 min**

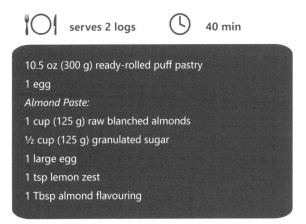

10.5 oz (300 g) ready-rolled puff pastry

1 egg

Almond Paste:

1 cup (125 g) raw blanched almonds

½ cup (125 g) granulated sugar

1 large egg

1 tsp lemon zest

1 Tbsp almond flavouring

 Preheat the oven to 400°F (205°C). Thaw the puff pastry (if it's frozen).

 For the almond paste: Add the almonds, sugar, almond flavouring, and zest to a food processor and grind for a few minutes until very fine. Add the egg and grind further until you have a fine paste. Store in fridge.

 Dust the counter with a little bit of flour. Unfold the puff pastry and carefully roll the dough out to a 9 x 9 in square (23 x 23 cm). Cut the dough in half and you will have two 9 x 4.5 in pieces.

 Roll the almond paste into two logs that are a bit shorter lengthways than the pastry. Place on the pastry. Wet the edges of the pastry slightly. Fold in the short ends first and then fold over long sides and press at the seams.

 Carefully turn the pastry over with the seam at the bottom and brush with the beaten egg. Bake for 25 min, or until the pastry turns golden brown. Remove from the oven and set aside to cool.

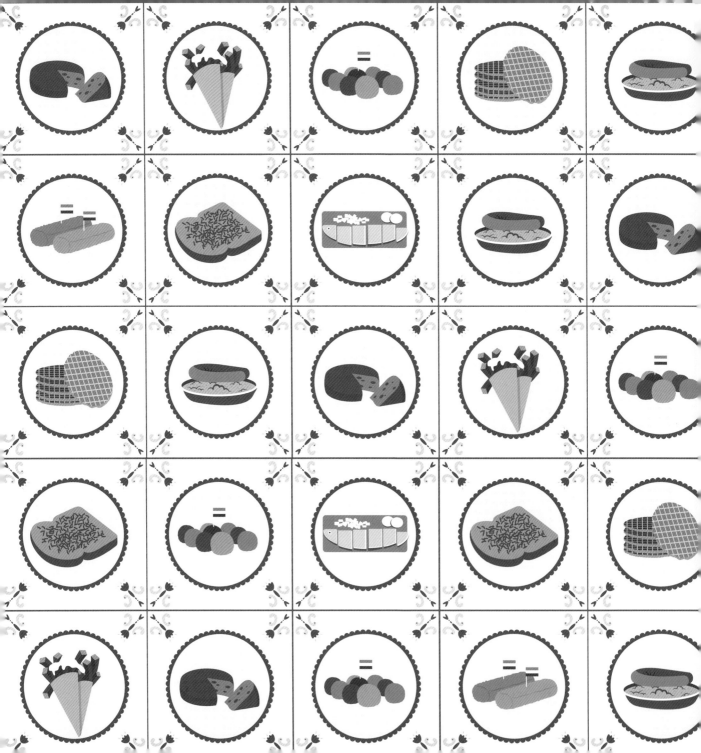

NEW YEAR'S
MADNESS

New Year's madness

The Dutch celebrate New Year's Eve, aptly called *Oud en Nieuw* ('old and new'), in a variety of unique ways. Aside from the notable tradition of—everyone and anyone—setting off elaborate firework displays across the nation, the Dutch also enjoy some truly delectable delights on the 31st of December.

If on New Year's Day, the doughy treats and boozy beverages from the night (or year) before have you feeling sluggish, you can always head to the seaside with thousands of your compatriots for a frigid dip! Of all the wacky Dutch traditions, I must say, this is definitely one of my favourites. What better way to start the new year than wading into the frigid winter waters of the North Sea alongside thousands of equally crazy Dutchies!

The New Year's dive/swim takes place in over 130 locations across the country. The seaside town of Scheveningen gathers the largest crowd, with normally over 10,000 arctic swimmers in attendance. Similar dives are held all over the world, however, the Netherlands boasts the most dive sites and the largest number of scantily-clad participants!

Now back to the food...let's start with the most celebrated of New Year's Eve nibbles: *oliebollen*! As soon as the temperature drops in the Netherlands, outdoor market stands and stalls start selling these sweet treats on nearly every corner. The smell alone will have your mouth watering before you even take the first bite. Who wouldn't love deep-fried balls of dough covered in powdered sugar?! The direct translation of *oliebol* is, you guessed it, "oily ball," the Dutch answer to the American doughnut. Due to its substantial nature, it is certainly not something you'd want to eat every week, however, on a cold winter day or evening, nothing quite celebrates the start of the festive season as a fresh *oliebol*!

Oliebollen
Dutch doughnuts

Oliebollen have a dumpling-like shape and resemble a homemade doughnut. Traditionally, these doughy lumps are made and eaten at midnight on New Year's Eve. However, *oliebollenkraam* (market stalls) pepper Dutch city streets from November onwards.

Historically speaking, they are said to have been first eaten by Germanic tribes in the Netherlands during Yuletide (December 26 to January 6). The first known Dutch recipe for *oliebollen*, then referred to as *oliekoecken* (oil cookies), dates from the 1667 Dutch cookbook, *"De Verstandige Kock"* (The Sensible Cook). Want to impress your New Year's Eve guests? Looking to bring a little bit of Holland into your home this holiday season? Give our fool-proof recipe a try!

 serves 20   **2 hrs 30 min**

2 cups all-purpose flour
1 cup lukewarm milk
1 package dry yeast
2 tsp salt
1 egg, lightly beaten
1½ cups raisins
1 apple, peeled, cored, and chopped
Oil (for deep frying)
Powdered sugar

 Add (a) ¼ of the milk to a large cup and stir in the yeast until dissolved.

 In a large bowl, combine the flour, salt, the remaining milk, and the egg. Then add yeast mixture, raisins, and the apple and mix thoroughly.

 Set aside and keep in a warm place until doubled.

 In a large pot, heat oil for frying. To check whether the oil is at the right temperature, stand the handle of a wooden spoon in the oil. If little bubbles form around it, the oil is ready.

 Using two metal spoons, shape balls out of the dough and drop them into the hot oil a few at a time.

 Deep fry for about 8 min (The *oliebollen* will sink to the bottom of the pan and should then pop right back up). Carefully remove the *oliebollen* and drain on a paper towel.

 Immediately sprinkle powdered sugar over the *oliebollen* and set aside to cool. Before serving you can sprinkle them with another dose of powdered sugar (optional).

Appelbeignets
Dutch apple fritters

With so many delicious Dutch desserts featuring apples, it's the perfect excuse to go apple picking in a local orchard (not that anyone ever needs an excuse to go apple picking!). That way, you'll be fully stocked for whatever apple recipe might appear, like *appelbeignets*! These Dutch apple fritters are made by slicing crisp, fresh apples into rings, coating them with batter, deep-frying them to golden perfection, and finishing them off with a sprinkling of cinnamon and powdered sugar. While they may look and sound similar to doughnuts, *appelbeignets* are even easier make and guaranteed to hit the spot.

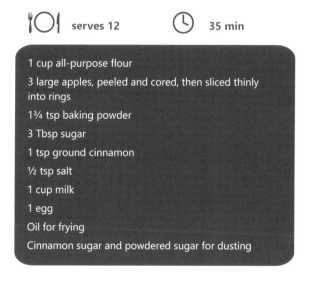 serves 12   35 min

1 cup all-purpose flour

3 large apples, peeled and cored, then sliced thinly into rings

1¾ tsp baking powder

3 Tbsp sugar

1 tsp ground cinnamon

½ tsp salt

1 cup milk

1 egg

Oil for frying

Cinnamon sugar and powdered sugar for dusting

 In a small bowl, lightly beat the milk and egg.

 In a large bowl, mix the flour, baking powder, sugar, cinnamon, and salt. Gradually mix the milk/egg mixture into the dry ingredients until the batter is thin enough to dip the apples, yet thick enough to stick. Add more flour or milk as needed to reach the necessary consistency. Let batter sit for 15 min.

 Meanwhile, heat the oil in a deep skillet or deep-fryer to 350°F (180°C).

 Line a baking sheet with paper towels. Take a couple slices at a time, dip the apple rings into the batter until fully coated, then add to the hot oil. Fry for 4 min, until puffy and golden brown, flipping them halfway. Carefully transfer on to the paper towels, drain and allow to cool a bit.

 Sprinkle the *appelbeignets* generously with cinnamon sugar, then a dusting of powdered sugar. Serve warm.

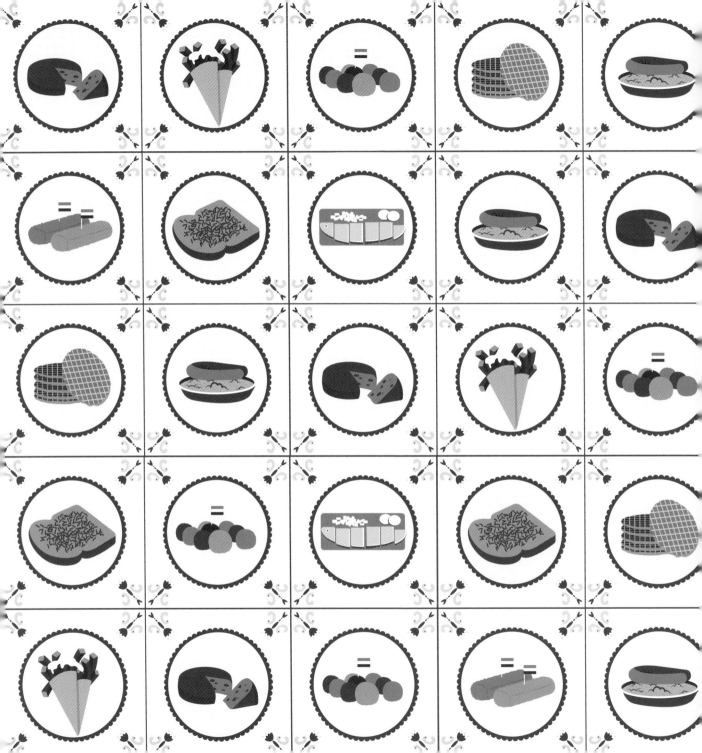

COLONIAL
CLASSICS

Dutch colonial houses in Willemstad, Curacao, Netherlands Antilles

Colonial classics

Although Dutch culture has its own heritage of traditional dishes originating from the Netherlands, Dutch cuisine also includes recipes rich with colonial influence, incorporating the exotic flavours and foods of the former Dutch colonies of Indonesia and Suriname.

The relationship between the Netherlands and Indonesia began with the establishment of the Dutch East India Company in the 17th century. After the spice trade successfully introduced new foods—such as sugar, spices, exotic fruits, and coffee—to Europe, Indonesia was colonised as the Dutch East Indies, and remained a Dutch colony until the mid-20th century.

Dutch colonial families learned about Indonesian cuisine through their immersion into the culture, as well as introducing European foods to Indonesia, though in the early colonial days it was only noble or highly educated Indonesian natives who were exposed to European cuisine. This knowledge of Indonesian cooking was brought back to Holland when Dutch colonial descendants—as well as Indonesian and Eurasian immigrants—returned to the Netherlands. In the same way, South American recipes found their way into Dutch cuisine when a great number of Surinamese immigrated to Holland in the 20th century, shortly before Suriname gained its independence from the Netherlands.

Among the many savoury Indonesian dishes that are now commonplace within the Dutch cooking repertoire are the popular *nasi goreng* (a spicy Indonesian fried rice made with chillies, garlic, chicken, and prawns and seasoned with a special sweet soy sauce), and *kipsaté*, marinated chicken satay with peanut sauce. Another Dutch favourite with colonial origins is the *Surinamese roti*, a hearty dish that combines curried chicken and potatoes with green beans and homemade flatbread. Today, many Indonesian and Surinamese dishes—both savoury and sweet—have become so well established within the Netherlands that they are as commonly cooked at home by Dutch families as even the most traditional fare.

"VOC Senior Merchant", by Aelbert Cuyp, c. 1640–60

Spekkoek
Indonesian layer cake

Spekkoek (also known as "thousand layer" cake) has a somewhat ambiguous history, as it originated in the Dutch East Indies during colonial times, making it hard to know whether this Indonesian layer cake was introduced by the Dutch or just adapted by them. Regardless, it is a popular dessert in both Indonesia and the Netherlands, despite being quite demanding to bake.

Spekkoek is made of numerous thin layers of cake, alternating between plain and spiced, a technique achieved by baking each layer individually, adding the next layer onto the already baked one until the cake is sufficiently tall enough. While time-consuming, the result is an impressive and decadent dessert that is best enjoyed thinly sliced and savoured with company during the holidays or on special occasions.

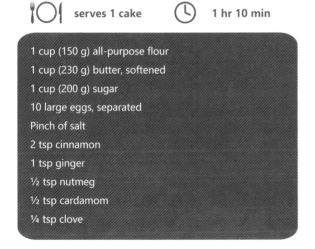 serves 1 cake   1 hr 10 min

1 cup (150 g) all-purpose flour
1 cup (230 g) butter, softened
1 cup (200 g) sugar
10 large eggs, separated
Pinch of salt
2 tsp cinnamon
1 tsp ginger
½ tsp nutmeg
½ tsp cardamom
¼ tsp clove

 1 In a large bowl, cream butter and sugar together with an electric mixer. Then whisk in the egg yolks. In another bowl, beat egg whites with salt until stiff and mix into the yolk mixture. Then mix in the flour.

 2 Divide batter into two bowls. Add the spices to one bowl and stir well.

 3 Line the bottom of a buttered 9 in (23 cm) round cake pan with wax paper and grease the wax paper with butter. Pour about ½ cup of the spice batter into the pan forming a thin layer. Place pan under a preheated broiler for 2 min, or until the layer is firm and very lightly browned (Don't leave unattended or you will regret it!).

 4 Pour 1/2 cup of the plain batter on top of the already cooked layer, spread thin and broil again for about 2 min until firm. Repeat layering (alternating between plain and spice batter) until all batter is used.

 5 Let cake cool, then remove from pan.

Nasi goreng
Indonesian fried rice

Many Asian countries have their own version of fried rice, and *nasi goreng* (which literally translates to "fried rice") belongs to Indonesia. It's considered the country's national dish, and is also quite popular in Malaysia and the Netherlands. There's no one standard recipe for *nasi goreng*, though there are some key ingredients—garlic, onion, chillies, chicken, prawns, and rice, of course! Another distinguishing element to *nasi goreng* is *kecap manis*, a sweet soy sauce that gives the dish a stronger flavour than other varieties of fried rice. Some versions of *nasi goreng* are topped with a fried egg, but in this recipe the eggs are cooked into an omelette, which is then stirred into the rice or served on top.

🍴 **serves 4**   🕐 **1 hr**

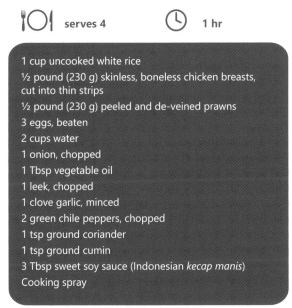

1 cup uncooked white rice
½ pound (230 g) skinless, boneless chicken breasts, cut into thin strips
½ pound (230 g) peeled and de-veined prawns
3 eggs, beaten
2 cups water
1 onion, chopped
1 Tbsp vegetable oil
1 leek, chopped
1 clove garlic, minced
2 green chile peppers, chopped
1 tsp ground coriander
1 tsp ground cumin
3 Tbsp sweet soy sauce (Indonesian *kecap manis*)
Cooking spray

 Cook the rice in a pot and then transfer into a large bowl. Refrigerate until cold.

 Apply cooking spray to a small pan and fry the eggs into a neat omelet (flip and fry both sides). Remove once done and slice the omelet into ½ in strips.

 In a wok (or large pan) heat the vegetable oil over high heat. Stir in the onion, garlic, leek, and chili peppers. Stir thoroughly for about 5 min, then mix in the chicken, prawns, coriander, and cumin. Cook and stir for approximately 5–10 min.

 Mix in the cold rice, sweet soy sauce, and omelet strips. Cook for another 5–10 min until shrimp are bright pink and chicken is cooked through (no longer pink in the center).

TIP   Instead of omelet strips, add a fried egg to each bowl of *nasi goreng*!

Kipsaté
Chicken satay with peanut sauce

Another Indo-Dutch favourite in the Netherlands is *kipsaté*, chicken satay with peanut sauce. *Satay* ("sate" in Indonesian) refers to any kind of seasoned meat that is skewered, grilled, and then served with a sauce, and is commonly found throughout Southeast Asia, as easily bought from street vendors as in sit-down restaurants.

In this recipe, chicken is marinated in soy sauce, lime zest, ginger, and garlic; placed on sate skewers and grilled; and served with a creamy, sweet, and spicy homemade peanut sauce, either drizzled on top of the chicken or served on the side for dipping.

serves 8 skewers   1 hr

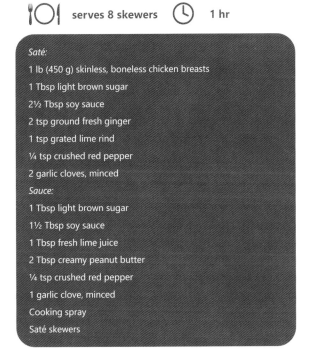

Saté:

1 lb (450 g) skinless, boneless chicken breasts

1 Tbsp light brown sugar

2½ Tbsp soy sauce

2 tsp ground fresh ginger

1 tsp grated lime rind

¼ tsp crushed red pepper

2 garlic cloves, minced

Sauce:

1 Tbsp light brown sugar

1½ Tbsp soy sauce

1 Tbsp fresh lime juice

2 Tbsp creamy peanut butter

¼ tsp crushed red pepper

1 garlic clove, minced

Cooking spray

Saté skewers

 Prepare the grill (chicken saté is best prepared using a grill).

 Cut chicken into 8 long strips (or into small chunks). Combine the chicken, sugar, soy sauce, ginger, lime, red pepper, and garlic in a large bowl. Let rest for 15–30 min.

 For the sauce, combine the sugar, soy sauce, lime juice, peanut butter, red pepper, and garlic in a medium bowl and keep stirring until the sugar dissolves.

 Thread chicken strips (or cubes) onto each of the 8 (8-in) skewers. Place chicken on grill rack coated with cooking spray and grill for 5 min on each side (or until chicken is cooked through). Serve skewers with sauce on top or on the side.

TIP   Ideal with fluffy white rice, a homemade cucumber salad, and crunchy prawn crackers!

Surinaamse roti
Surinamese roti

In addition to Indonesian inspiration, Dutch cuisine has also been influenced by the food of Suriname. This South American country was colonised by the Dutch in the late 17th century, and through the exchange of cultural influences, many Surinaamse dishes have made their way into Dutch cooking. One of those recipes is *Surinaamse roti*, a traditional dish of curried chicken and potatoes, green beans, and freshly baked flatbread.

🍴 serves 2   🕐 1 hr

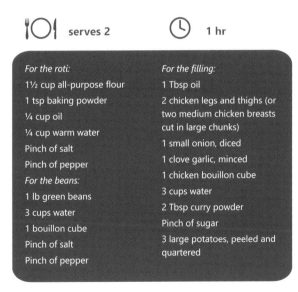

For the roti:
1½ cup all-purpose flour
1 tsp baking powder
¼ cup oil
¼ cup warm water
Pinch of salt
Pinch of pepper
For the beans:
1 lb green beans
3 cups water
1 bouillon cube
Pinch of salt
Pinch of pepper

For the filling:
1 Tbsp oil
2 chicken legs and thighs (or two medium chicken breasts cut in large chunks)
1 small onion, diced
1 clove garlic, minced
1 chicken bouillon cube
3 cups water
2 Tbsp curry powder
Pinch of sugar
3 large potatoes, peeled and quartered

 For the roti: Combine the flour, baking powder, salt, and pepper in a bowl, and gradually mix in the oil and water. Knead for about 5–10 min; keep adding the remaining flour until you have a dough that is smooth and elastic. Cover the bowl with some plastic film (or tinfoil) and let rise for about 20–30 min at room temperature.

 Cut and roll the dough into egg-sized balls. Flatten each dough ball using a rolling pin (lightly dust your working area beforehand). Heat up a large pan on high heat and bake the roti. Lightly coat the top with some sunflower oil, then turn it around. Repeat this 3 times or until nicely browned. Place them on a plate and cover with a towel.

 In a large pot (preferably Dutch oven), heat a bit of oil and brown the chicken on all sides. Add the garlic and the onion and let it cook for a couple of min. Mix in the pinch of sugar, water, curry and bouillon cube. Bring to a boil, then cover, lower the heat, and let simmer for 30 min. Add the potatoes (Make sure the water covers the potatoes completely. Otherwise, add more water.). Let simmer until the potatoes are done. Use a little bit of flour or cornstarch if the sauce is too thin.

 Cut the green beans into smaller pieces. Bring to a boil with the water and the bouillon cube until tender. Season with salt and pepper to taste.

 Serve the chicken, potatoes and beans on a plate with the warm roti on the side.

TIP This dish is a license to use your fingers! Break off a piece of *roti* to pick up the filling and soak up the sauce!

About us

About the Author

Colleen Geske is the blogger and best-selling author behind the hugely popular 'Stuff Dutch People Like' brand. Originally from Winnipeg, Canada, Colleen has called Amsterdam her home since 2004. Described as "blunt, provocative and wickedly funny", her blog and books offer an often satirical look at Dutch culture as seen through the eyes of an outsider.

About Stuff Dutch People Like

Stuff Dutch People Like is a celebration of all things Dutch. Started as a simple blog back in 2011, the Stuff Dutch People Like community now boasts a loyal following of over a half million fans in the Netherlands and around the world! The original Stuff Dutch People Like book was published in 2013 and became an instant international bestseller, with other books following suit! Visit us at
www.stuffdutchpeoplelike.com

Our books

Stuff Dutch People Like *(The Original)*

"Blunt, provocative and wickedly funny", *Stuff Dutch People Like* is a satirical look at Dutch culture as seen through the eyes of an outsider. From *Appelmoes* to *Zwarte Piet* and everything in between, *Stuff Dutch People Like* covers it all—and then some!

Stuff Dutch People Say

From the creators of *Stuff Dutch People Like* comes this hilarious companion. *Stuff Dutch People Say* delves deep into the linguistic world of the Lowlands, exploring what happens when Dutch and English collide. From funny Dutch words, incomprehensible Dutch expressions and hysterical examples of Dunglish, we've got you covered!

Stuff Dutch People Eat

Stuff Dutch People Eat is a comprehensive celebration of Dutch cuisine. Whether you're looking for festive sweets, traditional tastes or colonial classics, we've got something for every appetite! From breakfast straight through to dessert, *Stuff Dutch People Eat* will lead you through a culinary adventure spanning flavours—and centuries! Discover 40 easy-to-make recipes that are sure to restore your faith in the delightfully delicious Dutch kitchen! *Eet smakelijk*!

Stuff Dutch Moms Like

Stuff Dutch Moms Like investigates why Dutch moms are amongst the happiest in the world—and how they manage to have it all! Filled with hilarious anecdotes, tips and tricks, *Stuff Dutch Moms Like* takes an inside look at parenting in the Netherlands and the secrets to raising the happiest children in the world!

Index

Photo/Source Credits

Page	Attribution		Page	Attribution	
2	Sara Winter	Shutterstock	58	www.hollandfoto.net	Shutterstock
2	barmalini	Shutterstock	60	Pangfolio.com	Shutterstock
2	Justyna Pankowska	Shutterstock	61	Giancarlo Liguori	Shutterstock
2	HandmadePictures	Shutterstock	62	Sara Winter	Shutterstock
2	Mayabuns	Shutterstock	64	bonchan	Shutterstock
2	greatstockimages	Shutterstock	65	greatstockimages	Shutterstock
2	HeinzTeh	Shutterstock	66	p.studio66	Shutterstock
2	2xSamara.com	Shutterstock	68	Takeaway	CC BY-SA 3.0
2	r.martens	Shutterstock	76	katbaro	
2	bonchan	Shutterstock	78	hlphoto	Shutterstock
2	Roberts Photography	Shutterstock	80	Fanfo	Shutterstock
2	Sara Winter	Shutterstock	82	hlphoto	Shutterstock
2	Sara Winter	Shutterstock	86	Marc Venema	Shutterstock
2	picturepartners	Shutterstock	87	Olga Popova	Shutterstock
2	Ben Schonewille	Shutterstock	88	PHIL LENOIR	Shutterstock
2	Sara Winter	Shutterstock	89	Marc Venema	Shutterstock
2	MShev	Shutterstock	90	Takeaway	CC BY-SA 4.0
2	Sara Winter	Shutterstock	92	Fanfo	Shutterstock
2	Iryna Melnyk	Shutterstock	94	Sara Winter	Shutterstock
2	picturepartners	Shutterstock	96	Marc Venema	Shutterstock
2	Anna Baburkina	Shutterstock	98	Fanfo	Shutterstock
2	Marc Venema	Shutterstock	102	Giancarlo Liguori	Shutterstock
2	Elena Zajchikova	Shutterstock	104	Martijn van der Nat	Shutterstock
2	GreenArt Photography	Shutterstock	108	Nick_Nick	Shutterstock
2	hlphoto	Shutterstock	109	HG Photography	Shutterstock
6/7	Willy Van Cammeren		110	Martijn van Exel	(CC BY-SA 2.0
10	Iryna Melnyk	Shutterstock		https://www.flickr.com/photos/rhodes/6873340785	
12	aboikis	Shutterstock	112	Rikkert Harink	Shutterstock
13	Iryna Melnyk	Shutterstock	114	Sara Winter	Shutterstock
14	Sophie Idsinga		116	Sara Winter	Shutterstock
16	Takeaway	CC BY-SA 4.0	118	Anna Baburkina	Shutterstock
18	picturepartners	Shutterstock	120	Brent Hofacker	Shutterstock
20	MShev	Shutterstock	126	Sara Winter	Shutterstock
24	Roberts Photography	Shutterstock	127	Margreet de Groot	Shutterstock
26	Maren Winter	Shutterstock	128	Sara Winter	Shutterstock
27	goga18128	Shutterstock	130	HandmadePictures	Shutterstock
30	margouillat photo	Shutterstock	132	Charlotte Lake	Shutterstock
32	graletta	Shutterstock	134	graletta	Shutterstock
33	Martin Rettenberger	Shutterstock	138	Alexander Fritze	CC BY 2.0
34	Tom Gowanlock	Shutterstock		https://www.flickr.com/photos/afritze/4233067435/	
36	HandmadePictures	Shutterstock	140	InnervisionArt	Shutterstock
38	aquariagirl1970	Shutterstock	141	InnervisionArt	Shutterstock
42	Sara Winter	Shutterstock	142	Sara Winter	Shutterstock
44	Dutch Fish Marketing Board		144	Agnes Kantaruk	Shutterstock
45	Dutch Fish Marketing Board		148	Sorin Colac	Shutterstock
46	soulsoep	CC BY-SA 2.0	152	Aris Setya	Shutterstock
	https://www.flickr.com/photos/soepblog/2520848864		154	Hywit Dimyadi	Shutterstock
50	Sara Winter	Shutterstock	156	HeinzTeh	Shutterstock
52	ER_09	Shutterstock	158	Laig	CC BY-SA 3.0
54	CGissemann	Shutterstock			

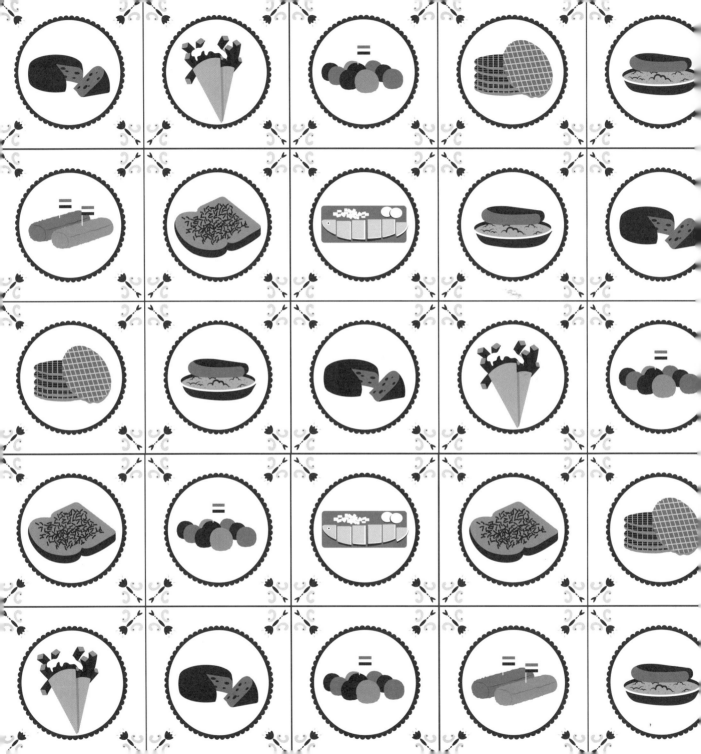